The Complete
Air Fryer

Cookbook for Beginners

1500-Day Delicious, Affordable & Super-Easy Air Fryer Recipes for Beginners and Advanced Users

Caitlin Naylor

© Copyright 2022 - All rights reserved.

The content contained within this book may not be reproduced, duplicated or transmitted without direct written permission from the author or the publisher.

Under no circumstances will any blame or legal responsibility be held against the publisher, or author, for any damages, reparation, or monetary loss due to the information contained within this book, either directly or indirectly.

Legal Notice:

This book is copyright protected. It is only for personal use. You cannot amend, distribute, sell, use, quote or paraphrase any part, or the content within this book, without the consent of the author or publisher.

Disclaimer Notice:

Please note the information contained within this document is for educational and entertainment purposes only. All effort has been executed to present accurate, up to date, reliable, complete information. No warranties of any kind are declared or implied. Readers acknowledge that the author is not engaged in the rendering of legal, financial, medical or professional advice. The content within this book has been derived from various sources. Please consult a licensed professional before attempting any techniques outlined in this book.

By reading this document, the reader agrees that under no circumstances is the author responsible for any losses, direct or indirect, that are incurred as a result of the use of the information contained within this document, including, but not limited to, errors, omissions, or inaccuracies.

Table of Contents

Introduction 7

The Fundamentals of an Air Fryer 8

What is an Air Fryer? 8
Benefits of Using an Air Fryer 9
A Step-by-Step Guide to Air Frying 10
Cleaning and Caring for an Air Fryer 11
Helpful Tips 11
FAQs 11

4-Week Diet Plan 12

Week 1 12
Week 2 12
Week 3 13
Week 4 13

Chapter 1 Breakfast Recipes 14

Milk and Pumpkin Donut Holes 14
Carrot and Golden Raisin Muffins 14
Avocado and Egg Burrito 15
Asparagus and Pepper Strata Sandwich .. 15
Cinnamon Crunchy Granola 15
Cranberry and Bran Flake Muffins 16
Chicken Sausages with Black Pepper 16
Jalapeño Egg Cups 16
Tasty Three-Berry Dutch Pancake 17
Cheddar Cheese and Buffalo Egg Cups ... 17
Simple Pumpkin Spice Muffins 17
Black Pepper and Cauliflower Avocado Toast
.... 18
Breakfast Sausage and Cheese Balls 18
Cheddar Cheesy Pepper Eggs 18
Tasty "Banana" Nut Cake 19
Vanilla Extract and Lemon Poppy Seed Cake
.... 19
Quick Bacon Strips 19
Simple French Toast Sticks 20

Crispy Ham Egg Cups 20
Veggie Cream Frittata 20
Vanilla Pancake Cake 21
Breakfast Sausage Stuffed with Poblanos 21
Simple Air Fryer "Hard-Boiled" Eggs 21
Cheddar Cheesy Cauliflower Hash Browns 22
Scrambled Eggs with Cheddar Cheese 22
Breakfast Bake with Loaded Cauliflower .. 22
Vanilla and Cinnamon Roll sticks 23
Crumbled Sausage and Scrambled Egg ... 23
Dried Fruit Beignets with Brown Sugar 24
Bacon, Egg, and Cheddar Cheese Roll Ups 24
Parmesan Veggie Frittata 25
Fried Salmon and Brown Rice Frittata 25

Chapter 2 Vegetable and Side Recipes .. 26

Butter Fried Cabbage 26
Sweet Potato Bites 26
Crispy Baby Potatoes 26
Versatile Bacon Potatoes with Green Beans
.... 27
Irresistible Carrots 27
Super-Fast Green Bean Fries 27
Delicious Street Corn 28
Crispy Okra 28
Healthy Kale Chips 28
Quick Corn Casserole 29
Perfect Potato Wedges 29
Golden Garlic Knots 29
Parmesan Cermini Mushrooms 30
Zest Fried Aasparagus 30
Delicious Butternut Squash 30
Tasty Bagel Brussels Sprouts 31
Crunchy Roasted Edamame 31
Wonderful Parmesan French Fries 31
Popular Buffalo Cauliflower 32
Scalloped Potato Slices 32

Sesame Carrots 32
Easy Courgette Chips 33
Crave-worthy Chicken Courgette Boats ... 33
Green Veggie Trio 33
Crisp Brussels Sprouts 34
Tasty Roasted Sweet Potatoes 34
Classic Parmesan French Fries 34
Versatile Potato Salad......................... 35
Butter Flaky Biscuits.......................... 35
Crispy Sweet Potato Fries..................... 35
Broccoli with Twice-baked Potatoes 36
Crispy Roasted Broccoli....................... 36
Green Tomatoes 37
Peppers with Garlic 37

Chapter 3 Fish and Seafood Recipes 38

Great Coconut Prawns with Orange Sauce 38
Fabulous Tuna Melt 38
Perfect Lemon Mahi-mahi..................... 39
Healthy Fried Tilapia........................... 39
Perfect Lemon Pepper Prawns................ 39
Sophisticated Fish Sticks...................... 40
Classic Crab Cakes 40
Gorgeous Honey-Balsamic Salmon 41
Delicious Prawns Kebabs...................... 41
Flavourful Hot Crab Dip....................... 41
Spanish Quick Paella 42
Perfect Seafood Tacos 42
Great Herbed Salmon 42
Delicious Catfish Bites 43
Family Favorite Thai-style Prawns Stir-fry 43
Delightful Crispy Fried Calamari 43
Easy Garlic Pesto Scallops.................... 44
Irresistible Chili-Lime Tilapia.................. 44
Easy and Delicious Coriander Butter Baked Mahi Mahi..................................... 44
Delicate Steamed Tuna 45
Easy Tuna Veggie Stir-Fry 45
Quick Scallops and Spring Veggies 45

Popular Fried Garlic Prawns 46
Easy French Mussels........................... 46
Great Cod with Creamy Mustard Sauce.... 47
Crisp Flounder au Gratin 47
Lemon-Herb Tuna Steaks 48
Zesty Lemon-Caper Salmon Burgers 48
Efficient Cod Piccata with Roasted Potatoes 49
Fresh Garlic-Dill Salmon with Tomatoes & Green Beans.................................... 49
Satisfying Parmesan Perch 50
Perfect Haddock Fish Fingers 50
Juicy Teriyaki Salmon 51
Distinct Cajun Prawns 51
Simple Snapper Scampi 52
Delicate Crab Ratatouille 52

Chapter 4 Poultry Recipes 53

Cajun Pepper & Chicken Kebabs............. 53
Pineapple Chicken Kebabs 53
Lemon Pepper Chicken Drumsticks 54
Stuffed Chicken Breast........................ 54
Mozzarella Chicken Pizza Crust.............. 54
Crusted Chicken................................ 55
Simple Chicken Fajitas 55
"Fried" Chicken 55
Creamy Chicken Corden Bleu Casserole... 56
Cheddar Jalapeño Popper Hasselback Chicken 56
Cajun Thyme Chicken Tenders 56
Chicken-Avocado Enchiladas 57
Mayo Chicken 57
Pepperoni and Chicken Pizza Bake 57
Teriyaki Chicken Wings 58
Thyme Roasted ChickenThyme Roasted Chicken 58
Lime Chicken Thighs........................... 58
Chicken Taquitos................................ 59

Crispy Chicken TendersCrispy Chicken Tender 59
Simple Turkey Tenderloin 59
Mexican Sheet Pan Chicken Supper 60
Apricot-Glazed Turkey Tenderloin 60
Turkey Burgers 60
Savory Sesame Chicken Tenders 61
Teriyaki Chicken and Broccoli Bowls 61
Turkey-bread Meatballs 62
Cheddar Stuffed Peppers 62
Parmesan-crumb Chicken 63
Balsamic Chicken and Veggies 63
Chicken Wraps 64
Spinach, Cheese and Chicken Meatballs .. 64
Breaded Chicken Strips 65
Dijon Roasted Turkey Breast 65
Spinach and Feta-Stuffed Chicken Breast 66
Black Pepper Chicken with Celery 66

Chapter 5 Beef, Pork, and Lamb Recipes 67

Pork Tenderloin with Mustard 67
Wrapped Pork Tenderloin 67
Butter Pork Chops 67
Marinated Steak Kebabs 68
Cheese-Stuffed Steak Burgers 68
Mozzarella Corn Dogs Mozzarella 68
Pork Chops Stuffed with Bacon and Cheese 69
Parmesan-Crusted Pork Chops 69
Marinated Ribeye Steak 69
Spicy Pork Spare Ribs 70
Mexican Shredded Beef 70
Pork Meatballs 70
London Steak 71
Italian Beef Meatballs 71
Roast Beef 71
Beef and Chorizo Burger 72
Spice-Rubbed Pork Loin 72

Tender Blackened Steak Nuggets 72
Cheese and Spinach Steak Rolls 73
Bacon and Cheese Burger Casserole 73
Juicy Baked Pork Chops 73
Crusted Buttery Beef Tenderloin 74
Southern-style Breaded Pork Chops 74
Lasagna Casserole 74
Air Fried Worcestershire Pork Belly 75
Classic Pulled Pork 75
Air Fryer Baby Back Ribs 75
Savory Latin American-style Pastries 76
Fajita Flank Steak Rolls 76
Tender Pork Spare Ribs 77
Tasty Seared Ribeye 77
Stuffed Peppers 78
Crispy Stir-fried Beef and Broccoli 78
Mozzarella-Stuffed Meatloaf 79
Simple Mini Meatloaf 79

Chapter 6 Snack and Starter Recipes 80

Fried Edamame 80
Spicy Fried Chickpeas 80
Fried Cinnamon and Sugar Peaches 80
Bacon-Wrapped Onion Rings 81
Mini Sweet Pepper Bacon Poppers 81
Fluffy Cheese Bread 81
Simple Five Spice Crunchy Edamame 81
Fried Black Bean Corn Dip 82
Crunchy Tortilla Chips 82
Courgette Chips 82
Thinly Sliced Beef Jerky 83
Italian Mozzarella Sticklets 83
Simple Bone Marrow Butter 83
Spicy Air-Fryer Sunflower Seeds 84
Air-Fryer Jalapeño Poppers 84
Roasted Jack-O'-Lantern Seeds with black pepper 84
Simple Baked Brie with Orange Marmalade and Spiced Walnuts 85

Air-Fryer Avocado Fries 85
Tasty Ranch Roasted Almonds 85
Crispy Chicken Wings 86
Prosciutto-Wrapped Asparagus 86
Fried Bacon-Wrapped Jalapeño Poppers .. 86
Fried Parmesan Chicken Wings 87
Spicy Fried Buffalo Chicken Dip.............. 87
Bacon Jalapeño Cheese Bread................ 87
Fried Cinnamon Apple Chips 88
Mozzarella-Stuffed Buffalo Meatballs....... 88
Mozzarella Cheese Sticks 88
Spinach Artichoke Dip.......................... 89
Simple Mozzarella Pizza Crust................ 89
Three-Meat Pizza 89
Bacon-Wrapped Brie 90
Smoky Roasted Almonds....................... 90
Italian Pepperoni Pizza Bread................. 90
Italian Salsa Verde............................... 91
Jalapeño Popper 91
Tasty Cauliflower Pizza Crusts................ 91
Almond and Mozzarella Cheese Pizza Rolls 92
Air-Fryer Barbecue Turnip Chips............. 92
Delicious Deviled Eggs 93
California Deviled Eggs 93
Mexican Fried Potato Skins 94
Bacon Cheeseburger Dip 94

Chapter 7 Dessert Recipes 95

Perfect Beignets 95
Quick and Easy Apple Pie Egg Rolls 95
Great Funnel Cake 96
Perfect Grilled Peaches 96
Classic Shortbread Sticks 96
Irresistible Churro Bites 97
Easy and Delicious Apple Fries 97
Easy S'more 97
Delicious Meringue Cookies................... 98
Great Chocolate-Stuffed Wontons 98
Quick and Easy Chocolate Mug Cake 98
Chocolate Pavlova 99
Tasty Banana Bread Muffins 99
Irresistible Raspberry Pavlova with Orange
Cream 100
Irresistible Carrot Cake Muffins 100
Simple Blueberry Hand Pies 101
Delicious Berry Cheese Cake 101
Low-carb Nutty Chocolate Cheesecake .. 102
Flavourful Chocolate Surprise Cookies ... 102
Fancy Chocolate Lava Cakes 103
Perfect Overload Dessert Pizza 103
Delicious Pumpkin Mug Cake................ 104
Delightful Almond Delights 104

Conclusion 105

Appendix 1 Measurement Conversion Chart 106

Appendix 2 Air Fryer Cooking Chart 107

Appendix 3 Recipes Index 108

Introduction

Congratulations! You're the proud owner of an air fryer, a small countertop electrical appliance that cooks delicious and crispy food using little to no oil.

Now, your mind is probably full of questions. How does an air fryer work? Does it actually fry food? How do you clean and maintain an air fryer? How do you use it? You'll get all the vital information about these types of cookers here. We'll help you discover what food you can cook in an air fryer. Basically, you can prepare all types of food in one, but with less or no oil, and the texture will be the same as fried food.

Using an air fryer is an excellent way to prepare food in your kitchen without using too many utensils. You simply gather all your ingredients, perhaps do some peeling and chopping, and then throw them into the air fryer. Adjust the cooking time and temperature according to the recipe instructions. The result? You'll have delicious and satisfying food with little to no effort.

From breakfasts to side dishes, mains, and desserts, you can cook all types of meals using an air fryer. It's pretty simple to use, and all buttons are user-friendly. The cleaning method is also incredibly easy. Just make sure you don't put the whole appliance into the dishwasher.

You'll get to spend more time with your family than in the kitchen, plus you'll feed them delicious, nutritious food. An air fryer is a perfect companion for busy people everywhere. Let's jump into everything you need to know about your new air fryer.

The Fundamentals of an Air Fryer

The air fryer cooks food by circulating hot air around it. One of its main benefits is its numerous cooking functions. It doesn't just fry food; it can bake and roast it. This handy appliance not only bakes cookies, cakes, and brownies but will create a scrumptious roast dinner, too. The best part? The air fryer cooks food with little to no oil. Plus, you don't need to spend ages washing up numerous pots, pans, baking trays, or bowls. Simply gather all your ingredients and prepare them. Throw them into the air fryer. Adjust the cooking time and temperature according to your recipe. Wait until the appliance beeps and your meal is ready to be served. The air fryer comes with all the essential accessories you'll need. You don't need to purchase a basket, baking tray, or other items. Simply put, an air fryer is simple to use and simple to clean!

What is an Air Fryer?

An air fryer is a user-friendly cooking appliance, easily used by anyone. It usually has seven cooking functions: crisp, fry, roast, grill, reheat, bake and dehydrate. It has simple-to-use operating buttons to control temperature, cooking time, start/stop, and power. The air fryer comes with useful accessories such as a reversible rack, air fryer basket, dehydrating rack, etc. By using its various programs, you can cook your favourite foods like French fries, pizza, casseroles, tacos, cakes, cookies, brownies, etc.

The air fryer has become a global phenomenon. In this cookbook, I've added air fryer recipes for the UK. All the ingredients are readily available in supermarkets and are written in UK measurements. The air fryer is the top trending appliance because of its health benefits and remarkable features. Now, let's look in more detail at its benefits!

Benefits of Using an Air Fryer

There are lots of benefits to using air fryer cooking appliances. These benefits include:

Food is cooked in very little to no oil:

The main advantage of this appliance is that it cooks food with little to no oil, leading to numerous health benefits. It's also an excellent choice for people looking to lose weight or reduce their fat intake.

Pretty simple cleaning process:

The air fryer comes with removable cooking parts. Before cleaning, you can remove them all and put them into the dishwasher. But remember: don't put the main unit in the dishwasher or submerge it in water. Doing so will damage your appliance. You can wipe the main unit with a damp cloth. When all the parts are dry, reassemble the unit.

Fast and safe:

The air fryer is an advanced cooking gadget. It cooks faster than other appliances and even the hob or oven. It's safe to use, doesn't produce too much steam or heat, and doesn't risk splashing oil like deep-fat fryers. You can adjust the cooking time and temperature according to the recipe instructions. The air fryer has a control panel with pre-set and user-friendly buttons, and you can adjust the time and temperature there.

No stove or oven needed:

An air fryer offers all types of cooking functions. You no longer need a stove or oven to bake or roast food; this handy appliance can even grill, fry, and dehydrate food.

Minimal mess:

When you use an air fryer, you'll discover that our kitchen will be easier to clean – no splattering oil or multiple dirty pans or trays to wash. And the air fryer basket is simple to clean as it's virtually non-stick and dishwasher-safe.

The perfect companion for busy people:

The air fryer is a perfect addition to your kitchen and offers simple cooking with minimal effort. Prepare the ingredients and add them to the air fryer basket. Adjust the cooking time, temperature, and desired functions and start cooking.

Large capacity:

The air fryer has a large capacity, meaning you can cook meals for the whole family. You can even roast an entire turkey for Christmas Day!

Time and money-saving:

An air fryer is ideal for cooking food in less time. It also saves you money; with an air fryer, you can make your favourite restaurant dishes or takeaway meals without the cost. Plus, you'll make these meals healthier by using less oil and ensuring your ingredients are freshly prepared.

A Step-by-Step Guide to Air Frying

First, clean it:

If you're using your air fryer for the first time, you'll need to ensure you clean it thoroughly. First, remove all packaging and labels from the appliance. Also, remove any accessories. Wash the air fryer basket and cooking tray in the dishwasher or hand wash them with warm soapy water. Clean the main unit inside and out with a soft cloth. When everything is dry, reassemble the appliance.

Choose a recipe from this cookbook:

Choose a recipe that catches your eye from this cookbook. I've included all types of recipes: Breakfast, Lunch, Dinner, Dessert, Snacks, etc. Have a good read through the book before picking a recipe you'd like to start with.

Buy fresh ingredients only:

It's a good idea to buy fresh ingredients, spices, veggies, fruits, and meat to get the best results. And buying fresh is better for your health too. Ensure you rinse all fruit and veg before cooking them.

Prepare the ingredients:

Before cooking, gather all your ingredients and measure them according to the recipe instructions. Try to cut veggies to the same size to ensure they cook evenly. If you want to marinate meat, do so in advance. If you're using frozen food, allow it to thaw if needed.

Preheat the unit if needed:

Some air fryer models need preheating, usually for the baking, roasting, and air frying functions. Please read the instructions carefully for your appliance and preheat it accordingly.

Spray the food with non-stick cooking spray:

Use high-quality cooking spray to spray your food before seasoning it. This will allow the seasoning to stick to the food and ensure that no smoke will be emitted from the appliance.

Select the cooking time, temperature, and desired cooking functions:

Select your desired function (such as Air Fry). Select the temperature and cooking time according to the recipe instructions. Place the food into the air fryer basket, baking dish, or cooking tray and close the lid/door of the main unit.

Flip the food if needed:

Some recipes will require food to be flipped over during cooking time. Some air fryer models will notify you when you need to turn your food. If not, you'll need to remember to do so yourself. Open the main unit's lid, shake the basket (or stir the food on the baking dish/tray), and close the lid. The cooking time will pause when you open the lid, and it will resume after closing it.

Remove the food when cooking time is complete:

Most air fryers' displays will let you know when the cooking time is complete. Remove the basket or tray from the appliance, then remove the food and transfer it to serving plates. Remember, the food will be piping hot!

Clean the air fryer after every use:

The air fryer basket is made with a non-stick coating and is dishwasher-safe. Rinse it under warm and soapy water first to remove any residue. Allow the appliance to cool before removing all accessories for cleaning.

Cleaning and Caring for an Air Fryer

Cleaning an air fryer is pretty simple. There are some instructions you should follow to maintain the appliance:

- Utensils such as steel wire brushes, metal utensils, and abrasive sponges can damage the surface of the main unit. Don't use them to remove leftover food from the air fryer basket, as it can damage the surface.
- Don't put the main unit into the dishwasher, as it will damage it beyond repair.
- Before cleaning, unplug the main unit from the socket. Don't immerse the unit in water.
- Clean the air fryer after every use. All parts of the air fryer are removable. Before cleaning, allow the main unit to cool, then remove the accessories using oven gloves or tongs.
- Use a damp cloth or non-abrasive sponge to clean the main unit's interior and exterior.
- To remove the grease from the air fryer basket, soak it overnight in warm soapy water.
- Use a soft scrub brush, washing-up liquid, baking soda, and a clean cloth for deep cleaning.

To deep clean:
- Unplug the appliance and allow it to cool for 30 minutes. Remove the pan and basket from the air fryer and wash them with hot water and soap. If you see grease on these parts, soak them in hot water for 10 minutes. Then, scrub with a non-abrasive sponge.
- Clean the basket's interior with washing-up liquid and wipe it with a damp cloth.
- Wipe the appliance with a moist or damp cloth carefully.
- If you see stubborn residue on the basket, mix baking soda and water and scrub the mixture into the grime with a soft brush.
- When all parts are dry, return them to the main unit.
- Reassemble the air fryer before the next use.

Helpful Tips

- Preheat the appliance according to the manufacturer's instructions. Add the food to the basket in one layer to produce tender and evenly-cooked food.
- For best results, remove food from the air fryer immediately after cooking to avoid burning and overcooking.
- Don't touch the surface of the main unit while cooking food. Use oven mitts or tongs. Remove the air fryer basket with oven mitts.
- Adjust the desired temperature and cooking time on the display screen. Press the start/stop button to start or stop cooking.
- When you open the lid during cooking, the cooking time will pause. When you close the top, the cooking time will resume.
- Use 1 tablespoon of oil for cooking vegetables.
- Flip the food if required by the recipe.
- Don't overfill the basket.
- Remove excess water from your ingredients, or the appliance will produce smoke.

FAQs

Why isn't the air fryer turning on?
Answer: Plug the appliance into another socket. Ensure that it's plugged in well.
Why does my air fryer shut off?
Answer: If you don't choose a cooking function within 10 minutes, the unit will turn off automatically.

4-Week Diet Plan

Week 1

Day 1:
Breakfast: Milk and Pumpkin Donut Holes
Lunch: Versatile Potato Salad
Snack: Spicy Fried Buffalo Chicken Dip
Dinner: Italian Beef Meatballs
Dessert: Quick and Easy Apple Pie Egg Rolls

Day 2:
Breakfast: Tasty Three-Berry Dutch Pancake
Lunch: Crispy Baby Potatoes
Snack: Bacon Cheeseburger Dip
Dinner: Cheddar Stuffed Peppers
Dessert: Irresistible Churro Bites

Day 3:
Breakfast: Quick Bacon Strips
Lunch: Tasty Bagel Brussels Sprouts
Snack: Spinach Artichoke Dip
Dinner: Popular Fried Garlic Prawns
Dessert: Perfect Beignets

Day 4:
Breakfast: Vanilla Pancake Cake
Lunch: Perfect Potato Wedges
Snack: Three-Meat Pizza
Dinner: Breaded Chicken Strips
Dessert: Low-carb Nutty Chocolate Cheesecake

Day 5:
Breakfast: Simple Air Fryer "Hard-Boiled" Eggs
Lunch: Crispy Sweet Potato Fries
Snack: Bacon-Wrapped Onion Rings
Dinner: Stuffed Peppers
Dessert: Irresistible Carrot Cake Muffins

Day 6:
Breakfast: Cinnamon Crunchy Granola
Lunch: Crispy Okra
Snack: Prosciutto-Wrapped Asparagus
Dinner: Perfect Lemon Mahi-mahi
Dessert: Delightful Almond Delights

Day 7:
Breakfast: Fried Salmon and Brown Rice Frittata
Lunch: Broccoli with Twice-baked Potatoes
Snack: Crispy Chicken Wings
Dinner: Teriyaki Chicken Wings
Dessert: Quick and Easy Chocolate Mug Cake

Week 2

Day 1:
Breakfast: Carrot and Golden Raisin Muffins
Lunch: Versatile Bacon Potatoes with Green Beans
Snack: Crunchy Tortilla Chips
Dinner: Simple Mini Meatloaf
Dessert: Fancy Chocolate Lava Cakes

Day 2:
Breakfast: Vanilla and Cinnamon Roll sticks
Lunch: Green Tomatoes
Snack: Mexican Fried Potato Skins
Dinner: Balsamic Chicken and Veggies
Dessert: Classic Shortbread Sticks

Day 3:
Breakfast: Breakfast Sausage and Cheese Balls
Lunch: Irresistible Carrots
Snack: Thinly Sliced Beef Jerky
Dinner: Delicious Prawns Kebabs
Dessert: Delicious Berry Cheese Cake

Day 4:
Breakfast: Cheddar Cheesy Pepper Eggs
Lunch: Peppers with Garlic
Snack: Tasty Ranch Roasted Almonds
Dinner: Spanish Quick Paella
Dessert: Perfect Grilled Peaches

Day 5:
Breakfast: Tasty "Banana" Nut Cake
Lunch: Delicious Butternut Squash
Snack: Spiced Walnuts
Dinner: Simple Turkey Tenderloin
Dessert: Delicious Pumpkin Mug Cake

Day 6:
Breakfast: Crispy Ham Egg Cups
Lunch: Sesame Carrots
Snack: Air-Fryer Avocado Fries
Dinner: Wrapped Pork Tenderloin
Dessert: Easy and Delicious Apple Fries

Day 7:
Breakfast: Cranberry and Bran Flake Muffins
Lunch: Tasty Roasted Sweet Potatoes
Snack: Spicy Air-Fryer Sunflower Seeds
Dinner: Chicken Taquitos
Dessert: Great Funnel Cake

Week 3

Day 1:
Breakfast: Avocado and Egg Burrito
Lunch: Quick Corn Casserole
Snack: Italian Salsa Verde
Dinner: Marinated Ribeye Steak
Dessert: Easy S'more

Day 2:
Breakfast: Parmesan Veggie Frittata
Lunch: Crunchy Roasted Edamame
Snack: Fried Black Bean Corn Dip
Dinner: Pork Meatballs
Dessert: Irresistible Raspberry Pavlova with Orange Cream

Day 3:
Breakfast: Jalapeño Egg Cups
Lunch: Healthy Kale Chips
Snack: Mozzarella Cheese Sticks
Dinner: Delicious Catfish Bites
Dessert: Low-carb Nutty Chocolate Cheesecake

Day 4:
Breakfast: Veggie Cream Frittata
Lunch: Sweet Potato Bites
Snack: Italian Pepperoni Pizza Bread
Dinner: Mayo Chicken
Dessert: Irresistible Carrot Cake Muffins

Day 5:
Breakfast: Cheddar Cheesy Cauliflower Hash Browns
Lunch: Parmesan Cermini Mushrooms
Snack: Delicious Deviled Eggs
Dinner: Easy French Mussels
Dessert: Delightful Almond Delights

Day 6:
Breakfast: Breakfast Bake with Loaded Cauliflower
Lunch: Crispy Roasted Broccoli
Snack: California Deviled Eggs
Dinner: Mozzarella Chicken Pizza Crust
Dessert: Quick and Easy Chocolate Mug Cake

Day 7:
Breakfast: Bacon, Egg, and Cheddar Cheese Roll Ups
Lunch: Super-Fast Green Bean Fries
Snack: Italian Mozzarella Sticklets
Dinner: Flavourful Hot Crab Dip
Dessert: Fancy Chocolate Lava Cakes

Week 4

Day 1:
Breakfast: Asparagus and Pepper Strata Sandwich
Lunch: Green Veggie Trio
Snack: Bacon-Wrapped Brie
Dinner: Turkey-bread Meatballs
Dessert: Classic Shortbread Sticks

Day 2:
Breakfast: Simple Pumpkin Spice Muffins
Lunch: Scalloped Potato Slices
Snack: Fluffy Cheese Bread
Dinner: Classic Pulled Pork
Dessert: Great Chocolate-Stuffed Wontons

Day 3:
Breakfast: Simple French Toast Sticks
Lunch: Popular Buffalo Cauliflower
Snack: Bacon Jalapeño Cheese Bread
Dinner: Lime Chicken Thighs
Dessert: Delicious Meringue Cookies

Day 4:
Breakfast: Dried Fruit Beignets with Brown Sugar
Lunch: Zest Fried Aasparagus
Snack: Mini Sweet Pepper Bacon Poppers
Dinner: Irresistible Chili-Lime Tilapia
Dessert: Simple Blueberry Hand Pies

Day 5:
Breakfast: Chicken Sausages with Black Pepper
Lunch: Crisp Brussels Sprouts
Snack: Jalapeño Popper
Dinner: Italian Roasted Whole Chicken
Dessert: Quick and Easy Apple Pie Egg Rolls

Day 6:
Breakfast: Scrambled Eggs with Cheddar Cheese
Lunch: Easy Courgette Chips
Snack: Smoky Roasted Almonds
Dinner: Juicy Baked Pork Chops
Dessert: Irresistible Churro Bites

Day 7:
Breakfast: Cheddar Cheese and Buffalo Egg Cups
Lunch: Delicious Street Corn
Snack: Simple Five Spice Crunchy Edamame
Dinner: Lemon-Herb Tuna Steaks
Dessert: Perfect Beignets

Chapter 1 Breakfast Recipes

Milk and Pumpkin Donut Holes

Prep Time: 15 minutes| **Cook Time:** 14 minutes| **Serves:** 12

125g whole-wheat pastry flour, plus more as needed
3 tablespoons packed brown sugar
½ teaspoon ground cinnamon
1 teaspoon baking powder
70g canned no-salt-added pumpkin purée (not pumpkin pie filling)
3 tablespoons low fat milk, plus more as needed
2 tablespoons unsalted butter, melted
1 egg white
Icing sugar (optional)

1. Mix the pastry flour, brown sugar, cinnamon, and baking powder in a medium bowl. 2. Beat the pumpkin, milk, butter, and egg white in a small bowl until they are combined. Add the pumpkin mixture to the dry ingredients and mix until combined. Add more flour or milk to form a soft dough. 3. Divide the dough into 12 pieces. Form each piece into a ball with floured hands. 4. Cut a piece of parchment paper or aluminum foil to fit inside the air fryer basket but about 2.5 cm smaller in diameter. Poke holes in the paper or foil and place it in the basket. 5. Put 6 donut holes into the basket, leaving some space around each. Air-fry at 180°C for 5 to 7 minutes, or until the donut holes reach an internal temperature of 95°C and are firm and light golden brown. 6. Let cool for 5 minutes. Remove from the basket and roll in icing sugar, if desired. Repeat with the remaining donut holes and serve.
Per Serving: Calories 59; Fat 1.69g; Sodium 8mg; Carbs 9.86g; Fibre 9.86g; Sugar 2.24g; Protein 1.87g

Carrot and Golden Raisin Muffins

Prep Time: 15 minutes| **Cook Time:** 12 to 17 minutes| **Serves:** 8

190g whole-wheat pastry flour
1 teaspoon baking powder
65g brown sugar
½ teaspoon ground cinnamon
1 egg
2 egg whites
180ml almond milk
3 tablespoons safflower oil
55g finely shredded carrots
45g golden raisins, chopped

1. Combine the baking powder, flour, brown sugar, and cinnamon in a medium bowl, and mix well. 2. Combine the egg, egg whites, almond milk, and oil in a small bowl and beat until combined. Then stir the egg liquid mixture into the dry ingredients just until combined. Don't overbeat; some lumps should be in the batter—that's just fine. 3. Stir the shredded carrot and chopped raisins gently into the batter. 4. Double up 16 foil muffin cups to make 8 cups. Put 4 of the cups into the air fryer and fill ¾ full with the batter. 5. Air fry at 160°C for 12 to 17 minutes or until the tops of the muffins spring back when lightly touched with your finger. 6. Repeat with the remaining muffin cups and the remaining batter. Cool the cooked muffins on a wire rack for 10 minutes before serving.
Per Serving: Calories 211; Fat 7.19g; Sodium 50mg; Carbs 33.67g; Fibre 3.1g; Sugar 15.16g; Protein 5.43g

Avocado and Egg Burrito

Prep Time: 10 minutes| **Cook Time:** 3 to 5 minutes| **Serves:** 4

2 hardboiled egg whites, chopped
1 hardboiled egg, chopped
1 avocado, peeled, pitted, and chopped
1 red pepper, chopped
3 tablespoons low-sodium salsa, plus additional for serving (optional)
1 (30g) slice low-sodium, low-fat American cheese, torn into pieces
4 low-sodium whole-wheat flour tortillas

1. Thoroughly mix the egg whites, egg, avocado, red pepper, salsa, and cheese in a medium bowl. 2. Flatten the tortillas on a work surface and evenly divide the filling among them. Fold in the edges and roll up. Secure the burritos with toothpicks if necessary. 3. Put the burritos in the air fryer basket at 200°C for 3 to 5 minutes, or until the burritos are light golden brown and crisp. 4. Serve with more salsa (if using).
Per Serving: Calories 204; Fat 14.67g; Sodium 86mg; Carbs 12g; Fibre 3.6g; Sugar 6.04g; Protein 8.17g

Asparagus and Pepper Strata Sandwich

Prep Time: 10 minutes| **Cook Time:** 14 to 20 minutes| **Serves:** 4

8 large asparagus spears, trimmed and cut into 5 cm pieces
40g shredded carrot
75g chopped red pepper
2 slices low-sodium whole-wheat bread, cut into 1 cm cubes
3 egg whites
1 egg
3 tablespoons low fat milk
½ teaspoon dried thyme

1. Combine the asparagus, carrot, red pepper, and 1 tablespoon of water in a 15 by 5 cm pan. Bake the veggies in the air fryer at 165°C for 3 to 5 minutes, or until crisp-tender. Drain well. 2. Add the bread cubes to the vegetables and gently toss. 3. Whisk the egg whites, egg, milk, and thyme in a medium bowl until frothy. 4. Pour the egg mixture into the pan. Bake the strata for 11 to 15 minutes, or until it is slightly puffy and set and the top starts to brown. 5. Serve.
Per Serving: Calories 100; Fat 3.42g; Sodium 151mg; Carbs 9.5g; Fibre 1.5g; Sugar 2.45g; Protein 7.64g

Cinnamon Crunchy Granola

Prep Time: 10 minutes| **Cook Time:** 5 minutes| **Serves:** 6

220g pecans, chopped
75g unsweetened coconut flakes
110g almond slivers
45g sunflower seeds
40g golden flaxseed
40g sugar-free chocolate chips
10g granular sweetener
2 tablespoons unsalted butter
1 teaspoon ground cinnamon

1. Mix all ingredients in a large bowl. 2. Place the mixture into a 6 x 2 cm round baking dish. Place dish into the air fryer basket. 3. Adjust the temperature to 160°C and set the timer for 5 minutes. 4. Allow to cool completely before serving.
Per Serving: Calories 429; Fat 39.21g; Sodium 205mg; Carbs 16.3g; Fibre 7.4g; Sugar 6.84g; Protein 9.19g

Cranberry and Bran Flake Muffins

Prep Time: 15 minutes| **Cook Time:** 15 minutes| **Serves:** 8

60g bran cereal flakes
125g plus 2 tablespoons whole-wheat pastry flour
3 tablespoons brown sugar
1 teaspoon baking powder
240ml low fat milk
3 tablespoons safflower oil or peanut oil
1 egg
55g dried cranberries

1. Mix the cereal, pastry flour, brown sugar, and baking powder in a medium bowl. 2. Whisk the milk, oil, and egg in a small bowl until they are combined. 3. Stir the egg mixture into the dry ingredients until just combined. 4. Stir in the cranberries. 5. Double up 16 foil muffin cups to make 8 cups. Put 4 cups into the air fryer and fill each three-fourths full with batter. Air fry at 160°C for about 15 minutes, or until the muffin tops spring back when lightly touched with your finger. 6. Repeat with the remaining muffin cups and batter. 7. Let cool on a wire rack for 10 minutes before serving.
Per Serving: Calories 176; Fat 7.85g; Sodium 68mg; Carbs 23.84g; Fibre 3g; Sugar 7.89g; Protein 4.81g

Chicken Sausages with Black Pepper

Prep Time: 15 minutes| **Cook Time:** 8 to 12 minutes| **Serves:** 8

1 Granny Smith apple, peeled and finely chopped
50g minced onion
3 tablespoons ground almonds
2 garlic cloves, minced
1 egg white
2 tablespoons apple juice
⅛ teaspoon freshly ground black pepper
450g chicken breast mince

1. Thoroughly mix the apple, onion, almonds, garlic, egg white, apple juice, and pepper in a medium bowl. 2. Gently work the chicken breast into the apple mixture with your hands until combined. 3. Form the mixture into 8 patties. Put the patties into the air fryer basket and air fry at 165°C for 8 to 12 minutes, or until the patties reach an internal temperature of 75°C on a meat thermometer. 4. Serve.
Per Serving: Calories 119; Fat 4.04g; Sodium 43mg; Carbs 4.1g; Fibre 0.7g; Sugar 2.63g; Protein 12.56g

Jalapeño Egg Cups

Prep Time: 10 minutes| **Cook Time:** 10 minutes| **Serves:** 2

4 large eggs
20g chopped pickled jalapeños
40g full-fat cream cheese
60g shredded sharp Cheddar cheese

1. Beat the eggs, then pour into four silicone muffin cups in a medium bowl. 2. Place jalapeños, cream cheese, and Cheddar in a large microwave-safe bowl. Microwave for 30 seconds and stir. Take a spoonful, approximately ¼ of the mixture, and place it in the centre of one of the egg cups. Repeat with remaining mixture. 3. Place egg cups into the air fryer basket. 4. Adjust the temperature to 160°C and set the timer for 10 minutes. 5. Serve warm.
Per Serving: Calories 286; Fat 23.78g; Sodium 425mg; Carbs 10.39g; Fibre 0.1g; Sugar 6.49g; Protein 7.89g

Tasty Three-Berry Dutch Pancake

Prep Time: 10 minutes| **Cook Time:** 12 to 16 minutes| **Serves:** 4

2 egg whites
1 egg
60g whole-wheat pastry flour
120ml low fat milk
1 teaspoon pure vanilla extract
1 tablespoon unsalted butter, melted
150g sliced fresh strawberries
75g fresh blueberries
60g fresh raspberries

1. Use an eggbeater or hand mixer to quickly mix the egg whites, egg, pastry flour, milk, and vanilla in a medium bowl until well combined. 2. Grease the bottom of a 15 by 5 cm pan with the melted butter with a pastry brush. Immediately pour in the batter and put the basket back in the fryer. Air fry at 165°C for 12 to 16 minutes, or until the pancake is puffed and golden brown. 3. Then remove the pan from the air fryer; the pancake will fall. Top with the strawberries, blueberries, and raspberries. 4. Serve immediately.
Per Serving: Calories 194; Fat 5.29g; Sodium 70mg; Carbs 30.12g; Fibre 3.9g; Sugar 16.79g; Protein 7.88g

Cheddar Cheese and Buffalo Egg Cups

Prep Time: 10 minutes| **Cook Time:** 15 minutes| **Serves:** 2

4 large eggs
50g full-fat cream cheese
2 tablespoons buffalo sauce
35g shredded sharp Cheddar cheese

1. Crack eggs into two (10cm) ramekins. 2. Mix cream cheese, buffalo sauce, and Cheddar in a small microwave-safe bowl. Microwave the sauce mixture for 20 seconds and then stir well. Add a spoonful into each ramekin on top of the eggs. 3. Place ramekins into the air fryer basket. 4. Adjust the temperature to 160°C and set the timer for 15 minutes. 5. Serve warm.
Per Serving: Calories 320; Fat 23.4g; Sodium 553mg; Carbs 4.6g; Fibre 0.3g; Sugar 2.8g; Protein 21.8g

Simple Pumpkin Spice Muffins

Prep Time: 10 minutes| **Cook Time:** 15 minutes| **Serves:** 6

95g blanched finely ground almond flour
10g sweetener
½ teaspoon baking powder
55g unsalted butter, softened
65g pure pumpkin purée
½ teaspoon ground cinnamon
¼ teaspoon ground nutmeg
1 teaspoon vanilla extract
2 large eggs

1. Mix almond flour, sweetener, baking powder, butter, pumpkin purée, cinnamon, nutmeg, and vanilla in a large bowl. 2. Gently stir in eggs. 3. Evenly pour the batter into six silicone muffin cups. Place muffin cups into the air fryer basket, working in batches if necessary. 4. Adjust the temperature to 150°C and set the timer for 15 minutes. 5. When completely cooked, a toothpick inserted in centre will come out mostly clean. 6. Serve warm.
Per Serving: Calories 295; Fat 25.61g; Sodium 344mg; Carbs 6.8g; Fibre 2.9g; Sugar 1.31g; Protein 13.11g

Black Pepper and Cauliflower Avocado Toast

Prep Time: 15 minutes| **Cook Time:** 8 minutes| **Serves:** 2

1 (300g) steamer bag cauliflower
55g shredded mozzarella cheese
1 ripe medium avocado
1 large egg
¼ teaspoon ground black pepper
½ teaspoon garlic powder

1. Cook cauliflower as the package instructed. Remove the cauliflower from the bag and place them into a cheesecloth or clean towel to remove any excess moisture. 2. Place the cauliflower into a large bowl and then mix together with egg and mozzarella. Cut a piece of parchment paper to fit your air fryer basket. Separate the cauliflower mixture into two servings, and place it on the parchment in two mounds. Press out the cauliflower mounds into a ½ cm-thick rectangle. Place the parchment into your air fryer basket. 3. Adjust the temperature to 205°C and set the timer for 8 minutes. 4. Flip the cauliflower halfway through the cooking time. 5. When the timer beeps, remove the parchment and allow the cauliflower to cool for 5 minutes. 6. Cut the avocado open and then remove the pit. Scoop out the inside, place it in a medium bowl, and mash it with garlic powder and pepper. Spread onto the cauliflower. Serve immediately.
Per Serving: Calories 233; Fat 17.01g; Sodium 222mg; Carbs 10.98g; Fibre 7.4g; Sugar 1.44g; Protein 12.56g

Breakfast Sausage and Cheese Balls

Prep Time: 10 minutes| **Cook Time:** 12 minutes| **Serves:** 4

455g pork breakfast sausage
55g shredded Cheddar cheese
25g full-fat cream cheese, softened
1 large egg

1. Mix the pork breakfast sausage, shreded cheddar cheese, cream cheese, and 1 egg in a large bowl. Form the mixture into sixteen (2.5cm) balls. Place the balls evenly into your air fryer basket. 2. Adjust the temperature setting to 205°C and set the timer for 12 minutes. 3. Shake the basket two or three times during cooking. Sausage balls will be browned on the outside and have an internal temperature of at least 60°C when completely cooked. 4. Serve warm.
Per Serving: Calories 548; Fat 43.83g; Sodium 2408mg; Carbs 1.92g; Fibre 0g; Sugar 0.44g; Protein 34.06g

Cheddar Cheesy Pepper Eggs

Prep Time: 10 minutes| **Cook Time:** 15 minutes| **Serves:** 4

4 medium green peppers
75g cooked ham, chopped
¼ medium onion, peeled and chopped
8 large eggs
115g mild Cheddar cheese

1. Cut the tops off each pepper. Remove the seeds and the white membranes with a small knife. Place ham and onion into each pepper. 2. Crack 2 eggs into each pepper. Top with 30 g cheese per pepper. Place into the air fryer basket. 3. Adjust the temperature to 200°C and set the timer for 15 minutes. 4. When fully cooked, peppers will be tender and eggs will be firm. Serve immediately.
Per Serving: Calories 152; Fat 9.84g; Sodium 292mg; Carbs 6.33g; Fibre 0.8g; Sugar 2.78g; Protein 9.96g

Tasty "Banana" Nut Cake

Prep Time: 15 minutes| **Cook Time:** 25 minutes| **Serves:** 6

95g blanched finely ground almond flour
10g powdered sweetener
2 tablespoons ground golden flaxseed
2 teaspoons baking powder
½ teaspoon ground cinnamon
55g unsalted butter, melted
2½ teaspoons banana extract
1 teaspoon vanilla extract
55g full-fat sour cream
2 large eggs
30g chopped walnuts

1. Mix almond flour, sweetener, flaxseed, baking powder, and cinnamon in a large bowl. 2. Stir in butter, banana extract, vanilla extract, and sour cream. 3. Add the 2 eggs to the mixture and gently stir until fully combined. Stir in the walnuts. 4. Pour into 15 cm nonstick cake pan and place into the air fryer basket. 5. Adjust the temperature to 150°C and set the timer for 25 minutes. 6. Cake will be golden and a toothpick inserted in centre will come out clean when fully cooked. Allow to fully cool to avoid crumbling.
Per Serving: Calories 276; Fat 23.92g; Sodium 27mg; Carbs 12.87g; Fibre 5.9g; Sugar 1.96g; Protein 9.15g

Vanilla Extract and Lemon Poppy Seed Cake

Prep Time: 10 minutes| **Cook Time:** 14 minutes| **Serves:** 6

95g blanched finely ground almond flour
10g powdered sweetener
½ teaspoon baking powder
55g unsalted butter, melted
60ml unsweetened almond milk
2 large eggs
1 teaspoon vanilla extract
1 medium lemon
1 teaspoon poppy seeds

1. Mix almond flour, sweetener, baking powder, butter, almond milk, eggs, and vanilla in a large bowl. 2. Slice the lemon in halves and then squeeze the juice into a small bowl. Add it to the batter. 3. Using a fine grater, zest the lemon and add 1 tablespoon zest to the batter and stir. Add poppy seeds to batter. 4. Pour batter into nonstick 15 cm round cake pan. Place pan into the air fryer basket. 5. When fully cooked, a toothpick inserted in centre will come out mostly clean. The cake will finish cooking and firm up as it cools. 6. Serve at room temperature.
Per Serving: Calories 235; Fat 20.62g; Sodium 20mg; Carbs 10.8g; Fibre 4.7g; Sugar 2.46g; Protein 7.85g

Quick Bacon Strips

Prep Time: 5 minutes| **Cook Time:** 12 minutes| **Serves:** 4

8 slices bacon

1. Place bacon strips into the air fryer basket. 2. Adjust the temperature to 205°C and set the timer for 12 minutes. 3. After 6 minutes, flip bacon and continue cooking time. 4. Serve warm.
Per Serving: Calories 88; Fat 6.2g; Sodium 355mg; Carbs 0.2g; Fibre 0g; Sugar 0g; Protein 5.8g

Simple French Toast Sticks

Prep Time: 6 minutes| **Cook Time:** 10 to 14 minutes| **Serves:** 4

3 slices whole-wheat bread, each cut into 4 strips
1 tablespoon unsalted butter, melted
1 egg
1 egg white
1 tablespoon low fat milk
1 tablespoon sugar
150g sliced fresh strawberries
1 tablespoon freshly squeezed lemon juice

1. Place the bread strips on a plate and drizzle with the melted butter. 2. Beat the egg, egg white, milk, and sugar in a shallow bowl. 3. Dip the whole-wheat bread into the egg mixture and place on a wire rack to let the batter drip off. 4. Air-fry half of the bread strips at 195°C for 5 to 7 minutes, turning the strips with tongs once during cooking, until golden brown. Repeat with the remaining strips. 5. Mash the strawberries and lemon juice with a fork or potato masher in a small bowl. 6. Serve the strawberry sauce with the French toast sticks.
Per Serving: Calories 137; Fat 5.43g; Sodium 152mg; Carbs 15.77g; Fibre 2.2g; Sugar 5.27g; Protein 6.62g

Crispy Ham Egg Cups

Prep Time: 5 minutes| **Cook Time:** 12 minutes| **Serves:** 2

4 (25g) slices deli ham
4 large eggs
2 tablespoons full-fat sour cream
40g diced green pepper
2 tablespoons diced red pepper
2 tablespoons diced white onion
60g shredded medium Cheddar cheese

1. Place one slice of ham on the bottom of four baking cups. 2. Whisk eggs with sour cream in a large bowl. Stir in green pepper, red pepper, and onion. 3. Pour the egg mixture into ham-lined baking cups. Top with Cheddar. Place cups into the air fryer basket. 4. Adjust the temperature to 160°C and set the timer for 12 minutes or until the tops are browned. 5. Serve warm.
Per Serving: Calories 174; Fat 10.64g; Sodium 623mg; Carbs 5.57g; Fibre 0.5g; Sugar 1.34g; Protein 13.85g

Veggie Cream Frittata

Prep Time: 15 minutes| **Cook Time:** 12 minutes| **Serves:** 4

6 large eggs
60g heavy whipping cream
45g chopped broccoli
40g chopped yellow onion
40g chopped green pepper

1. Whisk eggs and heavy whipping cream in a large bowl. Mix in broccoli, onion, and pepper. 2. Pour the egg-cream mixture into a 15 cm round oven-safe baking dish. Place the baking dish into the air fryer basket. 3. Adjust the temperature to 175°C and set the timer for 12 minutes. 4. Eggs should be firm and cooked fully when the frittata is done. 5. Serve warm.
Per Serving: Calories 145; Fat 10.6g; Sodium 114mg; Carbs 2.2g; Fibre 0.5g; Sugar 1g; Protein 10g

Vanilla Pancake Cake

Prep Time: 10 minutes| **Cook Time:** 7 minutes| **Serves:** 4

50g blanched finely ground almond flour
5g powdered sweetener
½ teaspoon baking powder
2 tablespoons unsalted butter, softened
1 large egg
½ teaspoon unflavoured gelatin
½ teaspoon vanilla extract
½ teaspoon ground cinnamon

1. Mix almond flour, sweetener, and baking powder in a large bowl. Add butter, egg, gelatin, vanilla, and cinnamon. Pour into 15 cm round baking pan. 2. Place pan into the air fryer basket. 3. Adjust the temperature to 150°C and set the timer for 7 minutes. 4. When the cake is completely cooked, a toothpick will come out clean. Cut cake into four and serve.
Per Serving: Calories 171; Fat 15.22g; Sodium 10mg; Carbs 7.39g; Fibre 3.6g; Sugar 1.13g; Protein 5.78g

Breakfast Sausage Stuffed with Poblanos

Prep Time: 15 minutes| **Cook Time:** 15 minutes| **Serves:** 4

225g spicy pork breakfast sausage meat
4 large eggs
100g full-fat cream cheese, softened
55g canned diced tomatoes and green chiles, drained
4 large poblano peppers
8 tablespoons shredded pepper jack cheese
115g full-fat sour cream

1. Crumble and brown the sausage meat in a medium frying pan over medium heat until no pink remains. Remove the pork sausage and then drain the fat from the pan. Crack the large eggs into the pan, scramble, and cook until no longer runny. 2. Place cooked sausage in a large bowl and fold in cream cheese. Mix in diced tomatoes and chiles. Gently fold in eggs. 3. Cut a 10 cm -13 cm slit in the top of each poblano and remove the seeds and white membrane with a small knife. Separate the filling into four servings and then spoon carefully into each pepper. Top each pepper with 2 tablespoons of pepper jack cheese. 4. Place each pepper into the air fryer basket. 5. Adjust the temperature to 175°C and set the timer for 15 minutes. 6. Peppers will be soft and cheese will be browned when ready. 7. Serve immediately with sour cream on top.
Per Serving: Calories 1282; Fat 100.28g; Sodium 2706mg; Carbs 16.49g; Fibre 0.8g; Sugar 5.75g; Protein 77.77g

Simple Air Fryer "Hard-Boiled" Eggs

Prep Time: 2 minutes| **Cook Time:** 18 minutes| **Serves:** 4

4 large eggs
240ml water

1. Place eggs into a 15 x 5 cm round baking-safe dish and pour water over eggs. Place dish into the air fryer basket. 2. Adjust the temperature to 150°C and set the timer for 18 minutes. 3. Store cooked eggs in the refrigerator until ready to use or peel and eat warm.
Per Serving: Calories 55; Fat 4.51g; Sodium 9mg; Carbs 0.61g; Fibre 0g; Sugar 0.1g; Protein 2.7g

Cheddar Cheesy Cauliflower Hash Browns

Prep Time: 20 minutes| **Cook Time:** 12 minutes| **Serves:** 4

1 (300g) steamer bag cauliflower
1 large egg
100g shredded sharp Cheddar cheese

1. Place the bag of cauliflower in your microwave and cook according to package instructions. Allow to cool completely and put cauliflower into a cheesecloth or kitchen towel and squeeze to remove excess moisture. 2. Mash cauliflower with a fork and add egg and cheese. 3. Cut a piece of parchment to fit your air fryer basket. Take ¼ of the mixture and form it into a hash brown patty shape. Place it onto the parchment and into the air fryer basket, working in batches if necessary. 4. Adjust the temperature setting to 205°C and set the timer for 12 minutes. 5. Flip the hash browns halfway through the cooking time. When completely cooked, they will be golden brown. 6. Serve immediately.
Per Serving: Calories 154; Fat 11g; Sodium 225mg; Carbs 4.7g; Fibre 1.7g; Sugar 1.8g; Protein 10g

Scrambled Eggs with Cheddar Cheese

Prep Time: 5 minutes| **Cook Time:** 15 minutes| **Serves:** 2

4 large eggs
2 tablespoons unsalted butter, melted
50g shredded sharp Cheddar cheese

1. Crack eggs into 10 cm round baking dish and whisk. Place dish into the air fryer basket. 2. Adjust the temperature to 205°C and set the timer for 10 minutes. 3. After 5 minutes, stir the eggs and add the butter and cheese. Let cook for 3 more minutes and stir again. 4. Allow eggs to finish cooking for an additional 2 minutes or remove if they are to your desired liking. 5. Use a fork to fluff. Serve warm.
Per Serving: Calories 179; Fat 16.74g; Sodium 21mg; Carbs 1.22g; Fibre 0g; Sugar 0.19g; Protein 5.85g

Breakfast Bake with Loaded Cauliflower

Prep Time: 15 minutes| **Cook Time:** 20 minutes| **Serves:** 4

6 large eggs
60g heavy whipping cream
160g chopped cauliflower
100g shredded medium Cheddar cheese
1 medium avocado, peeled and pitted
8 tablespoons full-fat sour cream
2 spring onions, sliced on the bias
12 slices bacon, cooked and crumbled

1. Whisk eggs and cream together in a medium bowl. Pour into a 15-cm round baking dish. 2. Add cauliflower and mix, then top with Cheddar. Place dish into the air fryer basket. 3. Adjust the temperature to 160°C and set the timer for 20 minutes. 4. When completely cooked, eggs will be firm and cheese will be browned. Slice into four pieces. 5. Slice avocado and divide evenly among pieces. Top each piece with 2 tablespoons sour cream, sliced spring onions, and crumbled bacon.
Per Serving: Calories 349; Fat 27.54g; Sodium 597mg; Carbs 11.48g; Fibre 4.2g; Sugar 1.54g; Protein 15.4g

Vanilla and Cinnamon Roll sticks

Prep Time: 10 minutes| **Cook Time:** 7 minutes| **Serves:** 4

110g shredded mozzarella cheese
25g full-fat cream cheese
30g blanched finely ground almond flour
½ teaspoon baking soda
10g granular sweetener, divided
1 teaspoon vanilla extract
1 large egg
2 tablespoons unsalted butter, melted
½ teaspoon ground cinnamon
3 tablespoons powdered sweetener
2 teaspoons unsweetened vanilla almond milk

1. Place mozzarella in a large microwave-safe bowl and break cream cheese into small pieces and place into bowl. Microwave for 45 seconds. 2. Stir in almond flour, baking soda, 5 g granular sweetener, and vanilla. A soft dough should form. Microwave the mix for additional 15 seconds if it becomes too stiff. 3. Mix egg into the dough, using your hands if necessary. 4. Cut a piece of parchment to fit your air fryer basket. Press the dough into an 20 cm × 13 cm rectangle on the parchment and cut into eight (2.5 cm) sticks. 5. Mix butter, cinnamon, and remaining granular sweetener in a small bowl. Brush half the butter mixture over the top of the sticks and place them into the air fryer basket. 6. Adjust the temperature to 205°C and set the timer for 7 minutes. 7. Halfway through the cooking time, flip the sticks and brush with remaining butter mixture. When done, sticks should be crispy. 8. To make glaze, whisk powdered sweetener and almond milk in a small bowl. Drizzle over cinnamon sticks. Serve warm.

Per Serving (2 sticks): Calories 97; Fat 4.04g; Sodium 296mg; Carbs 33.42g; Fibre 4.1g; Sugar 1.98g; Protein 8.57g

Crumbled Sausage and Scrambled Egg

Prep Time: 15 minutes| **Cook Time:** 15 minutes| **Serves:** 4

170g shredded mozzarella cheese
50g blanched finely ground almond flour
25g full-fat cream cheese
1 large whole egg
4 large eggs, scrambled
225g cooked breakfast sausage, crumbled
8 tablespoons shredded mild Cheddar cheese

1. Add mozzarella, almond flour, and cream cheese in a large microwave-safe bowl. Microwave for 1 minute. Stir until the mixture is smooth and forms a ball. Add the large egg and stir until dough forms. 2. Place dough between two sheets of parchment and roll out to ½ cm thickness. Cut the dough into four rectangles. 3. Mix scrambled eggs and cooked sausage together in a large bowl. Divide the mixture evenly among each piece of dough, placing it on the lower half of the rectangle. Sprinkle each with 2 tablespoons Cheddar. 4. Fold over the rectangle to cover the egg and meat mixture. Pinch, roll, or use a wet fork to close the edges completely. 5. Cut a piece of parchment to fit your air fryer basket and place the calzones onto the parchment. Place parchment into the air fryer basket. 6. Adjust the temperature to 195°C and set the timer for 15 minutes.7. Flip the calzones halfway through the cooking time. When done, calzones should be golden in colour. Serve immediately.

Per Serving: Calories 387; Fat 26.56g; Sodium 732mg; Carbs 7.03g; Fibre 2.6g; Sugar 2.02g; Protein 30.88g

Dried Fruit Beignets with Brown Sugar

Prep Time: 22 minutes| **Cook Time:** 5 to 8 minutes| **Serves:** 16

1 teaspoon active quick-rising dry yeast
80ml buttermilk
3 tablespoons brown sugar
1 egg
190g whole-wheat pastry flour
3 tablespoons chopped dried cherries
3 tablespoons chopped golden raisins
2 tablespoons unsalted butter, melted
Icing sugar, for dusting (optional)

1. Mix the yeast with 3 tablespoons of water in a medium bowl. Let it stand for 5 minutes, or until it bubbles. 2. Stir in the buttermilk, brown sugar, and egg until well mixed. 3. Stir in the pastry flour until combined. 4. With your hands, work the cherries and raisins into the dough. Let the mixture stand for 15 minutes. 5. Pat the dough into an 20 by 20 cm square and cut into 16 pieces. Gently shape each piece into a ball. 6. Drizzle the balls with the melted butter. Place them in a single layer in the air fryer basket so they don't touch. Cook these in batches. Air-fry at 165°C for 5 to 8 minutes, or until puffy and golden brown. 7. Dust with icing sugar before serving, if desired.

Per Serving: Calories 65; Fat 1.91g; Sodium 17mg; Carbs 10.34g; Fibre 1.3g; Sugar 2.07g; Protein 2.4g

Bacon, Egg, and Cheddar Cheese Roll Ups

Prep Time: 15 minutes| **Cook Time:** 15 minutes| **Serves:** 4

2 tablespoons unsalted butter
40g chopped onion
½ medium green pepper, seeded and chopped
6 large eggs
12 slices bacon
100g shredded sharp Cheddar cheese
145g mild salsa, for dipping

1. Melt butter in a medium frying pan over medium heat. Then add the chopped onion and pepper to the frying pan and sauté until fragrant and onions are translucent, about 3 minutes. 2. Whisk the eggs in a small bowl and pour the mixture into frying pan. Scramble the eggs with onions and peppers until fluffy and fully cooked, about 5 minutes. Remove from heat and set aside. 3. Place three slices of bacon side by side on work surface, overlapping about ½ cm. Place 35 g scrambled eggs in a heap on the side closest to you and sprinkle 25 g cup cheese on top of the eggs. 4. Tightly roll the bacon around the eggs and secure them with a toothpick as needed. Evenly put each roll into the air fryer basket. 5. Adjust the temperature to 175°C and set the timer for 15 minutes. Rotate the rolls halfway through the cooking time. 6. Bacon will be brown and crispy when completely cooked. Serve immediately with salsa for dipping.

Per Serving: Calories 165; Fat 13.6g; Sodium 264mg; Carbs 5.07g; Fibre 0.3g; Sugar 1.06g; Protein 5.34g

Parmesan Veggie Frittata

Prep Time: 10 minutes| **Cook Time:** 8 to 12 minutes| **Serves:** 4

75g chopped red pepper
50g minced onion
35g grated carrot
1 teaspoon olive oil
6 egg whites
1 egg
80ml low fat milk
1 tablespoon grated Parmesan cheese

1. Stir together the red pepper, onion, carrot, and olive oil in a 15 by 5 cm pan, and put the pan into the air fryer. Then cook for 4 to 6 minutes, shaking the basket once, until the vegetables are tender. 2. Meanwhile, beat the egg whites, egg, and milk in a medium bowl until they are combined. 3. Pour the egg mixture over the vegetables in the pan. Sprinkle with the Parmesan cheese and return the pan to the air fryer to bake at 175°C for 4 to 6 minutes more, or until the frittata is puffy and set. 4. Cut into 4 wedges and serve.
Per Serving: Calories 92; Fat 4.2g; Sodium 146mg; Carbs 4.08g; Fibre 0.5g; Sugar 2.68g; Protein 8.97g

Fried Salmon and Brown Rice Frittata

Prep Time: 15 minutes| **Cook Time:** 15 minutes| **Serves:** 4

Olive oil, for greasing the pan
1 egg
4 egg whites
½ teaspoon dried thyme
75g cooked brown rice
75g cooked, flaked salmon
15g fresh baby spinach
40g chopped red pepper
1 tablespoon grated Parmesan cheese

1. Rub a 15 by 5 cm pan with a bit of olive oil and set aside. 2. Beat the egg, egg whites, and thyme in a small bowl until they are well mixed. 3. Stir together the brown rice, salmon, spinach, and red pepper in the prepared pan. 4. Pour the egg mixture over the rice mixture and sprinkle with the Parmesan cheese. 5. Air fry at 160°C for about 15 minutes, or until the frittata is puffed and golden brown and serve.
Per Serving: Calories 57; Fat 2.84g; Sodium 106mg; Carbs 1.1g; Fibre 0.1g; Sugar 0.56g; Protein 6.36g

Chapter 2 Vegetable and Side Recipes

Butter Fried Cabbage

Prep Time: 5 minutes | **Cook Time:** 9 minutes | **Serves:** 2

Oil, for spraying
½ head cabbage, cut into bite-size pieces
2 tablespoons unsalted butter, melted
1 teaspoon granulated garlic
½ teaspoon coarse sea salt
¼ teaspoon freshly ground black pepper

1. Line the air fryer basket with parchment and spray some oil on it. 2. Combine the cabbage, butter, garlic, salt, and black pepper in a container. 3.Transfer the cabbage to the air fryer basket prepared before and spray some oil on it. 4.Turn to 190°C and cook for 5 minutes, toss, and cook for another 3 to 4 minutes.
Per Serving: Calories 136 ; Fat 10.23g; Sodium 625mg; Carbs 10.91g; Fibre 3g; Sugar 5.44g; Protein 2.62g

Sweet Potato Bites

Prep Time: 10 minutes | **Cook Time:** 25 minutes | **Serves:** 4

Oil, for spraying
3 medium sweet potatoes, peeled and cut into 2.5 cm pieces
2 tablespoons honey
1 tablespoon olive oil
2 teaspoons ground cinnamon

1. Line the air fryer basket with parchment and spray some oil on it. 2. Toss together the sweet potatoes, honey, olive oil, and cinnamon until evenly coated.3. Put the potatoes in the air fryer basket prepared before. 4. Cook them at 205°C for 25 minutes.
Per Serving: Calories 161; Fat 4.67g; Sodium 31mg; Carbs 29.77g; Fibre 3.5g; Sugar 15.15g; Protein 1.63g

Crispy Baby Potatoes

Prep Time: 10 minutes | **Cook Time:** 15 minutes | **Serves:** 4

Oil, for spraying
450g baby potatoes
50g grated Parmesan cheese, divided
3 tablespoons olive oil
2 teaspoons granulated garlic
½ teaspoon onion powder
½ teaspoon salt
¼ teaspoon freshly ground black pepper
¼ teaspoon paprika
2 tablespoons chopped fresh parsley, for garnish

1. Line the air fryer basket with parchment and spray some oil on it. 2. Wash the potatoes, pat dry with paper towels, and put in a container. 3. Mix together 25 g of Parmesan cheese, the olive oil, garlic, onion powder, salt, black pepper, and paprika. Coat the potatoes with the mixture. 4. Transfer the potatoes to the air fryer basket prepared before and spread them out in an even layer. 5. Cook them at 205°C for 15 minutes, and stir them after 7 to 8 minutes. 6. Sprinkle with the parsley and the remaining Parmesan cheese.
Per Serving: Calories 244; Fat 14.89g; Sodium 525mg; Carbs 22.45g; Fibre 2.7g; Sugar 0.96g; Protein 6.06g

Versatile Bacon Potatoes with Green Beans

Prep Time: 10 minutes | **Cook Time:** 25 minutes | **Serves:** 4

Oil, for spraying
900g medium russet potatoes, quartered
85g bacon bits
250g fresh green beans
1 teaspoon salt
½ teaspoon freshly ground black pepper

1. Line the air fryer basket with parchment and spray some oil on it. 2. Put the potatoes in the air fryer basket prepared before, and top them with the bacon bits and green beans, then prinkle them with the salt and black pepper and spray with oil. 3. Cook them at 180°C for 25 minutes, and stirring and spraying with oil after 12 minutes of cooking time, until the potatoes are easily pierced with a fork. 4. Serve warm.
Per Serving: Calories 305 ; Fat 7.1g; Sodium 966 mg; Carbs 50.05g; Fibre 6.4g; Sugar 1.96g; Protein 12.4g

Irresistible Carrots

Prep Time: 5 minutes | **Cook Time:** 12 minutes | **Serves:** 4

Oil, for spraying
385g baby Carrots
3 tablespoons olive oil
1 tablespoon unsalted butter, melted
1 tablespoon honey
½ teaspoon salt
¼ teaspoon freshly ground black pepper
⅛ teaspoon dried dill, for garnish

1. Line the air fryer basket with parchment and spray some oil on it. 2. Toss the carrots, olive oil, butter, honey, salt, and black pepper in a medium bowl until evenly coated. 3. Put the carrots in the air fryer basket prepared before. 4. Cook the carrots at 200°C for 12 minutes. 5. Transfer to a serving bowl, sprinkle with the dill, and enjoy.
Per Serving: Calories 167; Fat 13.4g; Sodium 349mg; Carbs 12.27g; Fibre 2.3g; Sugar 8.22g; Protein 0.93g

Super-Fast Green Bean Fries

Prep Time: 5 minutes | **Cook Time:** 5 minutes | **Serves:** 6

Oil, for spraying
450g fresh green beans, trimmed
60g plain flour
2 large eggs
110g panko bread crumbs
50g Parmesan cheese, plus more for serving (optional)
1 tablespoon granulated garlic

1. Line the air fryer basket with parchment and spray some oil on it. 2. Cut the green beans in half if any of the green beans are too long. 3. Put the green beans and flour in a zip-top plastic bag, seal, and shake well until evenly coated. 4. Whisk the eggs in a bowl. 5. Mix together the bread crumbs, Parmesan cheese, and garlic in another bowl. 6. Working in small batches, dip the green beans in the eggs, dredge in the panko mixture until evenly coated, and replace to the air fryer basket prepared before. 7.Cook them at 200°C for 5 minutes. 8. Sprinkle with additional Parmesan cheese before serving as you like.
Per Serving: Calories 132 ; Fat 5.23g; Sodium 184 mg; Carbs 15.93g; Fibre 1.9g; Sugar 1g; Protein 5.8g

Delicious Street Corn

Prep Time: 10 minutes | **Cook Time:** 15 minutes | **Serves:** 4

Oil, for spraying
4 ears corn, shucked
60g crumbled feta cheese
¼ teaspoon chili powder
¼ teaspoon salt
¼ teaspoon granulated garlic
⅛ teaspoon freshly ground black pepper
5g chopped fresh coriander
1 tablespoon lime juice

1. Line the air fryer basket with parchment and spray some oil on it. 2. Put the corn in the air fryer basket. 3. Cook them at 200°C for 10 minutes. 4. Sprinkle the corn with the feta cheese and continue to cook for 5 more minutes. 5. Transfer to a serving plate and sprinkle with the chili powder, salt, garlic, black pepper, and coriander. Just before serving, drizzle with the lime juice.

Per Serving: Calories 40; Fat 3.21g; Sodium 237mg; Carbs 1.63g; Fibre 0.2g; Sugar 0.48g; Protein 1.5g

Crispy Okra

Prep Time: 5 minutes | **Cook Time:** 12 minutes | **Serves:** 6

Oil, for spraying
1 large egg
60ml buttermilk
60g plain flour
80g polenta
½ teaspoon salt
¼ teaspoon freshly ground black pepper
450g okra, trimmed and cut into slices

1. Preheat the air fryer to 205°C. Line the air fryer basket with parchment and spray some oil on it. 2. Whisk the egg and buttermilk in a shallow bowl. 3. Mix together the flour, polenta, salt, and black pepper. 4. Toss the okra slices in the egg mixture, then dredge in the flour mixture until evenly coated, shaking off any excess. 5. Put the okra in the air fryer basket prepared before. For maximum crunch, spray some oil on it. 6. Cook them for 10 to 12 minutes, shaking and spraying with more oil after 4 minutes and after 7 minutes, until golden brown. 7. Sprinkle with additional salt as you like,.

Per Serving: Calories 131; Fat 2.08g; Sodium 221mg; Carbs 24.57g; Fibre 3.2g; Sugar 1.86g; Protein 4.27g

Healthy Kale Chips

Prep Time: 5 minutes | **Cook Time:** 5 minutes | **Serves:** 2

Oil, for spraying
80g loosely packed stemmed and torn kale
2 tablespoons olive oil
2 tablespoons dry Ranch seasoning
¼ teaspoon salt

1. Line the air fryer basket with parchment and spray some oil on it. 2. Toss the kale, olive oil, Ranch seasoning, and salt until evenly coated. 3. Put the Kale in the air fryer basket. 4. Cook them at 185°C for 4 to 5 minutes until crisp, shaking after 2 minutes. 5. Serve warm.

Per Serving: Calories 223; Fat 16.55g; Sodium 1001mg; Carbs 16.11g; Fibre 3.4g; Sugar 0.93g; Protein 4.14g

Quick Corn Casserole

Prep Time: 5 minutes | **Cook Time:** 15 minutes | **Serves:** 4

Nonstick baking spray with flour
500g frozen yellow corn
3 tablespoons flour
1 egg, beaten
60ml milk
120ml light cream
110g grated Swiss or Havarti cheese
Pinch salt
Freshly ground black pepper
2 tablespoons butter, cut in cubes

1. Spray a 15 x 5 cm baking pan with nonstick spray. 2. Combine the corn, flour, egg, milk, and light cream in a medium bowl, and mix until combined. Stir in the cheese, salt, and pepper. 3. Pour this mixture into the prepared baking pan. Dot with the butter. 4. Bake them at 160°C for 15 minutes. 5. Serve warm.
Per Serving: Calories 321; Fat 19.26g; Sodium 853mg; Carbs 26.53g; Fibre 2g; Sugar 4.43g; Protein 10.62g

Perfect Potato Wedges

Prep Time: 10 minutes | **Cook Time:** 20 minutes | **Serves:** 4

1.4 L water
4 large russet potatoes, sliced into wedges
2 teaspoons seasoned salt
120ml whole milk
60g all-purpose flour

1. In a large saucepan over medium-high heat, bring water to a boil. 2. Carefully put potato wedges into boiling water and cook 5 minutes. 3. Preheat the air fryer to 205°C. 4. Drain potatoes into a colander, then rinse under cold running water 1 minute until they feel cool to the touch. 5. Put potatoes in a container and sprinkle with seasoned salt. Pour milk into bowl, then toss wedges to coat. 6. Put flour on a large plate. Gently dredge each potato wedge in flour on both sides to lightly coat. 7. Put wedges in the air fryer basket and spritz both sides with cooking spray. Cook them for 15 minutes, turning after 10 minutes, until wedges are golden brown.
Per Serving: Calories 376; Fat 1.39g; Sodium 1202mg; Carbs 82.54g; Fibre 5.2g; Sugar 6.25g; Protein 10.42g

Golden Garlic Knots

Prep Time: 10 minutes | **Cook Time:** 15 minutes | **Serves:** 5

125g self-rising flour
245g plain full-fat Greek yogurt
80g salted butter, melted
1 teaspoon garlic powder
25g grated Parmesan cheese

1. Preheat the air fryer to 160°C. 2. In a container, mix flour and yogurt and let sit for 5 minutes. 3. Turn dough onto a lightly floured surface and gently knead about 3 minutes until it's no longer sticky. 4. Form dough into a rectangle and roll out until it measures 25 cm × 15 cm. Cut dough into ten 2.5 cm × 15 cm strips. 5. Tie each dough strip into a knot. Brush each knot with butter and sprinkle with garlic powder. 6. Put in the air fryer basket and cook for 8 minutes, turning after 6 minutes. 7. Let the dish cool for 2 minutes after cooking, sprinkle with Parmesan, and serve.
Per Serving: Calories 214; Fat 10.48g; Sodium 489mg; Carbs 23.16g; Fibre 0.7g; Sugar 3.53g; Protein 6.65g

Parmesan Cermini Mushrooms

Prep Time: 5 minutes | **Cook Time:** 15 minutes | **Serves:** 4

Oil, for spraying
450g cremini mushrooms, stems trimmed
2 tablespoons olive oil
2 teaspoons granulated garlic
1 teaspoon dried onion soup mix
½ teaspoon salt
¼ teaspoon freshly ground black pepper
35g grated Parmesan cheese, divided

1. Line the air fryer basket with parchment and spray some oil on it. 2. Toss the mushrooms with the olive oil, garlic, onion soup mix, salt, and black pepper until evenly coated. 3. Put the mushrooms in the air fryer basket prepared before. 4. Cook them at 185°C for 13 minutes. 5. Sprinkle half of the cheese over the mushrooms and cook for 2 more minutes. 6. Transfer the mushrooms to a serving bowl, add the remaining Parmesan cheese, and toss until evenly coated.
Per Serving: Calories 442; Fat 11.32g; Sodium 459 mg; Carbs 87.11g; Fibre 13.1g; Sugar 2.53g; Protein 13.32 g

Zest Fried Aasparagus

Prep Time: 5 minutes | **Cook Time:** 10 minutes | **Serves:** 4

Oil, for spraying
10 to 12 spears asparagus, trimmed
2 tablespoons olive oil
1 tablespoon granulated garlic
1 teaspoon chili powder
½ teaspoon ground cumin
¼ teaspoon salt

1. Line the air fryer basket with parchment and spray some oil on it. 2. Cut them in half if the asparagus are too long to fit easily in the air fryer. 3. Put the asparagus, olive oil, garlic, chili powder, cumin, and salt in a zip-top plastic bag, seal the bag, and toss them until evenly coated. 4. Put the asparagus in the air fryer basket prepared before. 5. Cook them at 200°C for 10 minutes, flipping them halfway through.
Per Serving: Calories 79; Fat 8.19g; Sodium 185mg; Carbs 1.49 g; Fibre 0.5g; Sugar 0.18g; Protein 0.47g

Delicious Butternut Squash

Prep Time: 15 minutes | **Cook Time:** 17 minutes | **Serves:** 4

Oil, for spraying
1 Butternut Squash, cut into 2.5 cm cubes
1 tablespoon olive oil
1 tablespoon maple syrup
1 teaspoon ground cinnamon

1. Line the air fryer basket with parchment and spray some oil on it. 2. Toss the squash with the olive oil, maple syrup, and cinnamon until evenly coated. 3. Put the squash in the air fryer basket prepared before. 4. Cook at 205°C for 17 minutes, shaking and stirring after 9 minutes, until tender.
Per Serving: Calories 70; Fat 4.55g; Sodium 2mg; Carbs 7.97g; Fibre 1g; Sugar 3.81 g; Protein 0.38g

Tasty Bagel Brussels Sprouts

Prep Time: 15 minutes | **Cook Time:** 15 minutes | **Serves:** 8

Oil, for spraying
675g Brussels Sprouts, trimmed
25g grated Parmesan cheese
25g finely chopped almonds
2 tablespoons olive oil
2 tablespoons Everything Bagel seasoning

1. Line the air fryer basket with parchment and spray some oil on it. 2. Bring a large pot of water to a boil over high heat. Add the brussels sprouts and cook until just softened, 8 to 10 minutes. Drain and let cool just long enough that you can handle them. 3. Cut the sprouts in half. Put the sprouts, Parmesan cheese, almonds, olive oil, and seasoning in a zip-top plastic bag, seal the bag, and toss until evenly coated. 4. Put the sprouts in the air fryer basket prepared before. 5. Cook them at 200°C for 12 to 15 minutes, and stir after 6 to 8 minutes. 6. Serve immediately.
Per Serving: Calories 146; Fat 5.46g; Sodium 185mg; Carbs 20.03g; Fibre 4.2g; Sugar 3.37g; Protein 6.27g

Crunchy Roasted Edamame

Prep Time: 5 minutes | **Cook Time:** 10 minutes | **Serves:** 4

Oil, for spraying
185g shelled Edamame
1 tablespoon olive oil
1 teaspoon hot sauce
½ teaspoon granulated garlic
Pinch salt, for serving

1. Line the air fryer basket with parchment and spray some oil on it. 2. In a medium bowl, toss together the edamame, olive oil, hot sauce, and garlic until evenly coated. 3. Put the Edamame in the air fryer basket. 4. Cook at 200°C for 10 minutes and stir after 5 minutes, until crunchy. If you want the edamame to be even crunchier, cook for 5 more minutes. 5. Add some salt to taste as you like..
Per Serving: Calories 135; Fat 8.53g; Sodium 111mg; Carbs 7.91g; Fibre 4.1g; Sugar 1.75g; Protein 8.48g

Wonderful Parmesan French Fries

Prep Time: 5 minutes | **Cook Time:** 10 minutes | **Serves:** 4.

230g frozen thin French fries
2 teaspoons olive oil
35g grated Parmesan cheese
½ teaspoon dried thyme
½ teaspoon dried basil
½ teaspoon salt

1. If there is any ice on the French fries, remove it. Put the French fries in the air fryer basket and drizzle with the olive oil. Toss them gently. 2. Air-fry them at 200°C for about 10 minutes, or until the fries are golden brown and hot, shaking the air fryer basket once during cooking time. 3. Immediately put the fries into a serving bowl and sprinkle with the Parmesan, thyme, basil, and salt. 4. Shake to coat and serve hot.
Per Serving: Calories 718; Fat 42.68g; Sodium 853mg; Carbs 78.1g; Fibre 11.5g; Sugar 0.01g; Protein 9.59g

Popular Buffalo Cauliflower

Prep Time: 10 minutes | **Cook Time:** 30 minutes | **Serves:** 4

Oil, for spraying
1 head cauliflower, cut into florets
2 tablespoons unsalted butter, melted
1 tablespoon olive oil
120ml buffalo sauce
50g almond flour or plain flour
3 tablespoons dried parsley
1 tablespoon granulated garlic
1 teaspoon seasoned salt

1. Line the air fryer basket with parchment and spray some oil on it. 2. Put the cauliflower, melted butter, olive oil, and buffalo sauce in a zip-top plastic bag, seal, and toss. 3. Mix the almond flour, parsley, garlic, and seasoned salt in a bowl. 4. Add the cauliflower to the flour mixture, and combine to coat. 5. Put half of the cauliflower in the air fryer basket prepared before. 6. Cook at 175°C for 15 minutes. After 7 or 8 minutes, shake and stir. 7. Do the same with the remaining cauliflower. 8. Serve warm.
Per Serving: Calories 214 ; Fat 8.95g; Sodium 973mg; Carbs 30.67g; Fibre 2.2 g; Sugar 13.24g; Protein 3.63g

Scalloped Potato Slices

Prep Time: 5 minutes | **Cook Time:** 20 minutes | **Serves:** 4

300g pre-sliced refrigerated potatoes
3 cloves garlic, minced
Pinch salt
Freshly ground black pepper
180g heavy cream

1. Layer the potatoes, garlic, salt, and pepper in a 20 cm x 20 cm x 4 cm baking pan. Slowly pour the cream over all. 2. Bake them at 195°C for 15 minutes, until the potatoes are golden brown on top and tender. Check their state and, if needed, bake for 5 minutes until browned.
Per Serving: Calories 139; Fat 8.46g; Sodium 492 mg; Carbs 14.47g; Fibre 1.7g; Sugar 1.24g; Protein 2.18g

Sesame Carrots

Prep Time: 5 minutes | **Cook Time:** 6 minutes | **Serves:** 4-6

455g baby carrots
1 tablespoon sesame oil
½ teaspoon dried dill
Pinch salt
Freshly ground black pepper
6 cloves garlic, peeled
3 tablespoons sesame seeds

1. Put the baby carrots in a medium bowl. Drizzle with sesame oil, add the dill, salt, and pepper, and toss to coat well. 2. Put the carrots in the air fryer basket of the air fryer. Roast them at 195°C for 8 minutes, shaking the air fryer basket once during cooking time. 3. Add the garlic to the air fryer basket. Roast them for 8 minutes, shaking the air fryer basket once during cooking time, or until the garlic and carrots are lightly browned. 4. Transfer to a serving bowl and sprinkle with the sesame seeds before serving.
Per Serving: Calories 77; Fat 4.93g; Sodium 111mg; Carbs 7.78g; Fibre 2.8g; Sugar 2.66g; Protein 1.66g

Easy Courgette Chips

Prep Time: 10 minutes | **Cook Time:** 12 minutes | **Serves:** 2

Oil, for spraying
1 medium courgette, cut into ½ cm-thick slices
50g grated Parmesan cheese
Pinch salt (optional)

1. Line the air fryer basket with parchment and spray some oil on it. 2. Put the courgette in a single layer in the air fryer basket. 3. Sprinkle the courgette with the Parmesan cheese, covering the tops of each chip. 4. Cook them at 185°C for 10 to 12 minutes, or until the cheese is dark golden brown. The courgette will crisp as it cools. 5. Sprinkle with the salt as you like.
Per Serving: Calories 166; Fat 13.78g; Sodium 645mg; Carbs 3.65 g; Fibre 0.1g; Sugar 0.02g; Protein 7.25g

Crave-worthy Chicken Courgette Boats

Prep Time: 5 minutes | **Cook Time:** 9 minutes | **Serves:** 4

Oil, for spraying
2 medium courgette, cut in half lengthwise
280g shredded rotisserie or leftover chicken
75g cream cheese, softened
60ml Ranch dressing
55g shredded Cheddar cheese
2 tablespoons buffalo sauce
55g shredded mozzarella cheese

1. Preheat the air fryer to 200°C. Line the air fryer basket with parchment and spray some oil on it. 2. Scrape out the inner flesh of the courgette, leaving about ½ cm all the way around, to create a boat. 3. Put the boats in the air fryer basket prepared before. 4. Cook them for 3 to 5 minutes, or until just starting to blister. 5. Mix together the chicken, cream cheese, ranch dressing, fheddar cheese, and buffalo sauce. 6. Spoon the chicken mixture into the boats, dividing evenly. Top each with mozzarella cheese. 7. Cook them for 4 minutes until the cheese is melted.
Per Serving: Calories 286; Fat 21.27g; Sodium 869mg; Carbs 6.7g; Fibre 0.5g; Sugar 4.54g; Protein17.82g

Green Veggie Trio

Prep Time: 6 minutes | **Cook Time:** 9 minutes | **Serves:** 4

180g Broccoli florets
200g green beans
1 tablespoon olive oil
1 tablespoon lemon juice
225g frozen baby peas
2 tablespoons Honey mustard
Pinch salt
Freshly ground black pepper

1.Put the Broccoli and green beans in the air fryer basket of the air fryer. Put 2 tablespoons water in the air fryer pan. Sprinkle the vegetables with the olive oil and lemon juice, and toss. 2. Steam them at 165°C for 6 minutes, then remove the air fryer basket from the air fryer and add the peas.3. Steam for 3 minutes or until the vegetables are hot and tender. 4.Transfer the vegetables to a serving dish and drizzle with the honey mustard and sprinkle with salt and pepper.
Per Serving: Calories 79; Fat 4.32g; Sodium 310mg; Carbs 7.91g; Fibre 3.7g; Sugar 1.85g; Protein 3.39g

Crisp Brussels Sprouts

Prep Time: 8 minutes | **Cook Time:** 20 minutes | **Serves:** 4

455g fresh Brussels Sprouts
1 tablespoon olive oil
½ teaspoon salt
⅛ teaspoon pepper
25g grated Parmesan cheese

1. Trim the bottoms from the brussels sprouts and pull off any discoloured leaves. Toss with the olive oil, salt, and pepper, and put in the air fryer basket. 2. Roast them at 165°C for 20 minutes, shaking the air fryer basket twice during cooking time. 3. Transfer the brussels sprouts to a serving dish and toss with the Parmesan cheese.
Per Serving: Calories 105; Fat 5.46g; Sodium 432mg; Carbs 11.16g; Fibre4.3g; Sugar 2.57g; Protein 5.64g

Tasty Roasted Sweet Potatoes

Prep Time: 5 minutes | **Cook Time:** 25 minutes | **Serves:** 4

2 sweet potatoes, peeled and cut into 2.5 cm cubes
1 tablespoon olive oil
Pinch salt
Freshly ground black pepper
½ teaspoon dried thyme
½ teaspoon dried marjoram
25 cm grated Parmesan cheese

1. Put the sweet potato cubes in the air fryer basket and drizzle with the olive oil, gently toss them. Sprinkle with the salt, pepper, thyme, and marjoram, and toss again. 2. Roast them at 165°C for 20 minutes, shaking the air fryer basket once during cooking time. 3. Remove the air fryer basket from the air fryer and shake the potatoes again. Sprinkle evenly with the Parmesan cheese and return to the air fryer. 4. Roast them for 5 minutes or until the potatoes are tender. 5. Serve warm.
Per Serving: Calories 57 ; Fat 5.17g; Sodium 210mg; Carbs 0.94g; Fibre 0g; Sugar 0.01g; Protein 1.86 g

Classic Parmesan French Fries

Prep Time: 5 minutes | **Cook Time:** 45 minutes | **Serves:** 4

3 large russet potatoes, peeled, trimmed, and sliced into 1 × 10 cm sticks
2½ tablespoons olive oil, divided
2 teaspoons minced garlic
½ teaspoon salt
¼ teaspoon ground black pepper
1 teaspoon dried parsley
25g grated Parmesan cheese

1. Put potato sticks in a container of cold water and let soak for 30 minutes. 2. Preheat the air fryer to 175°C. 3. Drain potatoes and gently pat dry. Put in a large, dry bowl. 4. Pour 2 tablespoons oil over potatoes; add garlic, salt, and pepper, then toss to fully coat. 5. Put fries in the air fryer basket and cook for 15 minutes, shaking the air fryer basket twice during cooking, until fries are golden and crispy on the edges. 6. Put fries into a clean medium bowl and drizzle with remaining ½ tablespoon oil. Sprinkle parsley and Parmesan over fries and toss to coat.
Per Serving: Calories 308; Fat 8.73g; Sodium 853mg; Carbs 51.63g; Fibre 3.7g; Sugar 1.88g; Protein 7.85g

Versatile Potato Salad

Prep Time: 5 minutes | **Cook Time:** 25 minutes | **Serves:** 4-6

900g tiny red or creamer potatoes, cut in half
1 tablespoon plus 80 ml olive oil
Pinch salt
Freshly ground black pepper
1 red pepper, chopped
2 green onions, chopped
80ml lemon juice
3 tablespoons Dijon or yellow mustard

1. Put the potatoes in the air fryer basket and drizzle with 1 tablespoon of the olive oil. Sprinkle with salt and pepper. 2. Roast them at 175°C for 25 minutes, shaking twice during cooking time, until the potatoes are tender and light golden brown. 3. Put the pepper and green onions in a container. 4. Combine the remaining 80 ml of olive oil, the lemon juice, and mustard, and mix well with a whisk in a small bowl. 5. When the potatoes are cooked, add them to the bowl with the peppers and top with the dressing. Toss gently to coat. 6. Let cool for 20 minutes. Stir gently again and serve or refrigerate and serve later.
Per Serving: Calories 263; Fat 16.15g; Sodium 492mg; Carbs 27.44g; Fibre 3.5g; Sugar 13.12g; Protein 3.75g

Butter Flaky Biscuits

Prep Time: 10 minutes | **Cook Time:** 15 minutes | **Serves:** 8

55g salted butter
250g self-rising flour
¼ teaspoon salt
65ml whole milk

1. Preheat the air fryer to 160°C. Cut parchment paper to fit the air fryer basket. 2. Put butter in the freezer 10 minutes. In a container, mix flour and salt. 3. Grate butter into bowl and use a wooden spoon to evenly distribute. Add milk and stir until a soft dough forms. 4. Turn dough onto a lightly floured surface. Gently press and flatten dough until mostly smooth and uniform. Gently roll into an 20 cm × 25 cm rectangle. Use a sharp knife dusted in flour to cut dough into eight squares. 5. Put biscuits on parchment paper in the air fryer basket, working in batches as necessary, and cook them for 15 minutes until golden brown on the top and edges and feel firm to the touch. 6. Let the dish cool 5 minutes before serving.
Per Serving: Calories 163; Fat 4.76g; Sodium 853mg; Carbs 25.83g; Fibre 0.8g; Sugar 2.7g; Protein 3.74g

Crispy Sweet Potato Fries

Prep Time: 35 minutes | **Cook Time:** 10 minutes | **Serves:** 4

2 large sweet potatoes, trimmed and sliced into ½ cm × 10 cm sticks
1 tablespoon olive oil
½ teaspoon salt

1. Put sweet potato sticks in a container of cold water and let soak for 30 minutes. 2. Preheat the air fryer to 195°C. 3. Drain potatoes and gently pat dry. Put in a large, dry bowl. Drizzle with oil and sprinkle with salt, then toss to fully coat. 4. Put fries in the air fryer basket and cook for 10 minutes, shaking the air fryer basket three times during cooking, until fries are tender and golden brown. 5. Serve warm.
Per Serving: Calories 111; Fat 3.51g; Sodium 323mg; Carbs 18.64g; Fibre 3g; Sugar 5.83g; Protein 1.81g

Broccoli with Twice-baked Potatoes

Prep Time: 10 minutes | **Cook Time:** 46 minutes | **Serves:** 4

Oil, for spraying
2 medium russet potatoes
1 tablespoon olive oil
20g Broccoli florets
1 tablespoon sour cream
1 teaspoon granulated garlic
1 teaspoon onion powder
60g shredded Cheddar cheese

1. Line the air fryer basket with parchment and spray some oil on it. 2. Wash the potatoes and pat dry with paper towels. Rub the outside of the potatoes with the olive oil and put them in the air fryer basket prepared before. 3. Cook them at 205°C for 40 minutes. Let cool just enough to handle after cooking, then cut the potatoes in half lengthwise. 4. Put the Broccoli in a microwave-safe bowl, cover with water, and microwave on high for 5 to 8 minutes. Drain and set aside. 5. Scoop out most of the potato flesh and replace to a medium bowl. 6. Add the sour cream, garlic, and onion powder and stir until the potatoes are mashed. 7. Spoon the potato mixture back into the hollowed potato skins, mounding it to fit. Top with the broccoli and cheese. Return the potatoes to the air fryer basket. 8. Cook at 205°C for 3 to 6 minutes until the cheese has melted. 9. Serve warm.
Per Serving: Calories 198 ; Fat 5.22g; Sodium 42mg; Carbs 34.61g; Fibre 2.6g; Sugar 1.39g; Protein 4.59g

Crispy Roasted Broccoli

Prep Time: 10 minutes | **Cook Time:** 15 minutes | **Serves:** 4

For Broccoli
Oil, for spraying
450g broccoli florets
2 teaspoons peanut oil
1 tablespoon minced garlic
½ teaspoon salt
For Sauce
2 tablespoons soy sauce
2 teaspoons honey
2 teaspoons sriracha
1 teaspoon rice vinegar

1. Line the air fryer basket with parchment and spray some oil on it. 2. Toss together the Broccoli, peanut oil, garlic, and salt until evenly coated. 3. Spread out the Broccoli in an even layer in the air fryer basket. 4. Cook at 205°C for 15 minutes, stirring halfway through. 5. In a small microwave-safe bowl, combine the soy sauce, honey, sriracha, and rice vinegar, and microwave them in the oven on high for about 15 seconds. Stir to combine. 6. Transfer the broccoli to a serving bowl and add the sauce. Gently toss and enjoy.
Per Serving: Calories 92 ; Fat 5.38 g; Sodium 449 mg; Carbs 8.83 g; Fibre 3.3g; Sugar 4.89g; Protein 4.31 g

Green Tomatoes

Prep Time: 5 minutes | **Cook Time:** 8 minutes | **Serves:** 4

Oil, for spraying
2 green (unripe) tomatoes, cut into slices
½ teaspoon salt
¼ teaspoon freshly ground black pepper
60g plain flour
2 large eggs
120ml buttermilk
110g panko bread crumbs
160g polenta

1. Turn on the air fryer and preheat it to 205°C. Line the air fryer basket with parchment and spray some oil on it. 2. Season the tomato slices with salt and black pepper. 3. Put the flour on a shallow plate. 4. Whisk the eggs and buttermilk in a small bowl. 5. Combine the bread crumbs and polenta on another shallow plate. 6. Dredge the tomato slices in the flour, dip in the egg mixture, and coat with the panko bread crumbs on both sides. 7. Put the tomato slices in the air fryer basket and spray some oil on it. 8. Cook them for for 5 minutes, flip, and cook for 3 more minutes.
Per Serving: Calories 292; Fat 5.11g; Sodium 145mg; Carbs 52.36g; Fibre 2.9g; Sugar 2.68g; Protein 8.64g

Peppers with Garlic

Prep Time: 8 minutes | **Cook Time:** 22 minutes | **Serves:** 4

1 red pepper
1 yellow pepper
1 orange pepper
1 green pepper
2 tablespoons olive oil, divided
½ teaspoon dried marjoram
Pinch salt
Freshly ground black pepper
1 head garlic

1. Slice the peppers into 2.5 cm strips. 2. Toss the peppers with 1 tablespoon of the oil. Sprinkle on the marjoram, salt, and pepper, and toss again. 3. Cut off the top of the garlic head and put the cloves on an oiled square of aluminum foil. Drizzle with the remaining olive oil. Wrap the garlic in the foil. 4. Put the wrapped garlic in the air fryer and roast them at 165°C for 15 minutes, then add the peppers. Roast for 7 minutes or until the peppers are tender and the garlic is soft. Transfer the peppers to a serving dish. 5. Remove the garlic from the air fryer and unwrap the foil. When cool enough to handle, squeeze the garlic cloves out of the papery skin and mix with the peppers.
Per Serving: Calories 88; Fat 7g; Sodium 123 mg; Carbs 6.35 g; Fibre 1g; Sugar 1.75 g; Protein 1.25 g

Chapter 3 Fish and Seafood Recipes

Great Coconut Prawns with Orange Sauce

Prep Time: 15 minutes | **Cook Time:** 15 minutes | **Serves:** 4

40g unsweetened grated coconut
30g whole-wheat bread crumbs
30g whole-wheat flour
¼ teaspoon smoked paprika
¼ teaspoon freshly ground black pepper
¼ teaspoon salt
1 egg
1 teaspoon water
455g medium prawns, peeled and deveined
Extra-virgin olive oil, in a spray bottle, for greasing
2 tablespoons maple syrup
½ teaspoon rice vinegar
⅛ teaspoon red pepper flakes
60ml freshly squeezed orange juice
1 teaspoon cornflour

1. Turn on and preheat the air fryer to 175°C. 2. Mix in a shallow bowl together the coconut, bread crumbs, flour, paprika, black pepper, and salt. 3. In a separate shallow bowl, whisk together the egg and water. 4. Dip a prawns into the egg, shaking off any excess. Dip it into the coconut–bread crumb mixture, making sure to coat it completely. Do the same with the rest of the prawns. 5. Put the prawns in the air fryer basket in a single layer and spray the tops with olive oil. 6. Cook for 5 minutes. Turn over the prawns and continue cooking for another 2 to 3 minutes. 7. In a small saucepan, combine the maple syrup, vinegar, and red pepper flakes and stir until combined. Mix in a small bowl together the orange juice and cornflour. Add it to the saucepan, and bring to a boil over medium heat. Cook, stirring frequently, for 5 minutes. Remove from the heat and let sit for 5 minutes.
Per Serving: Calories 190; Fat 4.05g; Sodium 871mg; Carbs 18.66g; Fibre 1.4g; Sugar 8.57g; Protein 19.32g

Fabulous Tuna Melt

Prep Time: 3 minutes | **Cook Time:** 10 minutes | **Serve:** 1 sandwich

Oil, for spraying
½ (125g) can tuna, drained
1 tablespoon mayonnaise
¼ teaspoon granulated garlic, plus more for garnish
2 teaspoons unsalted butter
2 slices sandwich bread
2 slices cheddar cheese

1. Line the air fryer basket with parchment and sprinkle with oil lightly. 2. Mix in a medium bowl together the tuna, mayonnaise, and garlic. 3. Spread 1 teaspoon of butter on each slice of bread and place one slice butter-side down in the air fryer basket prepared before. 4. Put on the top a slice of cheese, the tuna mixture, another slice of cheese, and the other slice of bread, butter-side up. 5. Cook for 5 minutes at 205°C, flip, and cook for 5 more minutes. 6. Sprinkle the sandwich with another garlic before cutting in half and serving.
Per Serving: Calories 540; Fat 35.46g; Sodium 880mg; Carbs 21.2g; Fibre 1.3g; Sugar 2.56g; Protein 34.28g

Perfect Lemon Mahi-mahi

Prep Time: 5 minutes | **Cook Time:** 14 minutes | **Serves:** 2

Oil, for spraying
2 (150g) mahi-mahi fillets
1 tablespoon lemon juice
1 tablespoon olive oil
¼ teaspoon salt
¼ teaspoon freshly ground black pepper
1 tablespoon chopped fresh dill
2 lemon slices

1. Line the air fryer basket with parchment and sprinkle with oil lightly. 2. Put the mahi-mahi in the air fryer basket prepared before. 3. Whisk the lemon juice and olive oil in a small bowl, then evenly brush the mahi-mahi with the mixture. 4. Sprinkle the mahi-mahi with the salt and black pepper and put on the top the dill. 5. Cook the mahi-mahi at 205°C for 12 to 14 minutes 6. Replace the food to plates, and top each with one lemon slice. Enjoy.
Per Serving: Calories 349; Fat 24.92g; Sodium 709mg; Carbs 13.53g; Fibre 6.1g; Sugar 2.08g; Protein 20.31g

Healthy Fried Tilapia

Prep Time: 15 minutes | **Cook Time:** 6 minutes | **Serves:** 4

Oil, for spraying
110g panko bread crumbs
2 tablespoons Old Bay seasoning
2 teaspoons granulated garlic
1 teaspoon onion powder
½ teaspoon salt
¼ teaspoon freshly ground black pepper
1 large egg
4 tilapia fillets

1. Turn on and preheat the air fryer to 205°C. Line the air fryer basket with parchment and sprinkle with oil lightly. 2. Mix the bread crumbs, Old Bay, garlic, onion powder, salt, and black pepper in a shallow bowl. 3. Whisk the egg in a small bowl. 4. Coat the tilapia in the egg, then dredge in the bread crumb mixture until completely coated. 5. Put the tilapia in the air fryer basket prepared before. sprinkle with oil lightly. 6. Cook the fillets for 4 to 6 minutes until they have an internal temperature of 60°C. .
Per Serving: Calories 166; Fat 4.61g; Sodium 397mg; Carbs 6.19g; Fibre 0.6g; Sugar 0.57g; Protein 24.98g

Perfect Lemon Pepper Prawns

Prep Time: 15 minutes | **Cook Time:** 8 minutes | **Serves:** 2

Oil, for spraying
300g medium raw prawns, peeled and deveined
3 tablespoons lemon juice
1 tablespoon olive oil
1 teaspoon lemon pepper
¼ teaspoon paprika
¼ teaspoon granulated garlic

1.Turn on and preheat the air fryer to 205°C. Line the air fryer basket with parchment and sprinkle with oil lightly. 2. Toss in a medium bowl together the prawns, lemon juice, olive oil, lemon pepper, paprika, and garlic until evenly coated. 3. Put the prawns in the air fryer basket prepared before. 4. Cook the prawns for 6 to 8 minutes until pink and firm. 5. Serve hot.
Per Serving: Calories 216; Fat 10.86g; Sodium 965mg; Carbs 5.53g; Fibre 0.5g; Sugar 1.76g; Protein 23.75g

Sophisticated Fish Sticks

Prep Time: 10 minutes | **Cook Time:** 15 minutes | **Serves:** 4

For Tartar Sauce
440g mayonnaise
2 tablespoons dill pickle relish
1 tablespoon dried minced onions
For Fish Sticks
Oil, for spraying
450g tilapia fillets
60g plain flour
215g panko bread crumbs
2 tablespoons Creole seasoning
2 teaspoons granulated garlic
1 teaspoon onion powder
½ teaspoon salt
¼ teaspoon freshly ground black pepper
1 large egg

1. Whisk the mayonnaise, pickle relish, and onions in a small bowl. Cover the bowl with plastic wrap and refrigerate them until ready to serve. You can make this sauce ahead of time, the flavours will intensify as it chills. 2. Turn on and preheat the air fryer to 175°C. Line the air fryer basket with parchment and sprinkle with oil lightly. 3. Cut the fillets into equal-size sticks and place them in a zip-top plastic bag. 4. Add the flour to the bag, seal, and shake well until evenly coated. 5. Mix the bread crumbs, Creole seasoning, garlic, onion powder, salt, and black pepper in a shallow bowl. 6. Whisk the egg in a small bowl. 7. Dip the fish sticks in the egg, then dredge in the bread crumb mixture until completely coated. 8. Put the fish sticks in the air fryer basket prepared before, and lightly sprinkle them with oil. Do not overcrowd. 9. Cook the fish sticks for 12 to 15 minutes until browned. Serve the dish with tartar sauce.
Per Serving: Calories 651; Fat 43.12g; Sodium 1735mg; Carbs 30.79g; Fibre 3.1g; Sugar 4.89g; Protein 34.16g

Classic Crab Cakes

Prep Time: 10 **minutes** | **Cook Time:** 20 minutes | **Serves:** 4

2 large eggs
2 tablespoons mayonnaise
1 teaspoon Dijon mustard
1 teaspoon Worcestershire sauce
1½ teaspoons Old Bay seasoning
25g finely chopped spring onions
450g lump crabmeat
55g panko bread crumbs
Oil, for spraying
1 lemon, cut into wedges

1. Mix the eggs, mayonnaise, mustard, Worcestershire sauce, Old Bay, and spring onions in a large bowl. 2. Add the crabmeat and bread crumbs and fold gently until combined. 3. Cover the bowl with plastic wrap and refrigerate for at least 1 hour. 4. Turn on and preheat the air fryer to 175°C. Line the air fryer basket with parchment and sprinkle with oil lightly. 5. Divide the mixture into 8 equal portions and shape into 2.5 cm thick patties. Put 4 patties in the air fryer basket prepared before and sprinkle with oil lightly. 6. Cook the patties for 5 minutes, flip, spray with oil again, and cook for 5 more minutes. Do the same with the remaining patties. 7. Squeeze a lemon wedge over each crab patty.
Per Serving: Calories 80; Fat 6.01g; Sodium 112mg; Carbs 4.5g; Fibre 0.5g; Sugar 0.96g; Protein 2.4g

Gorgeous Honey-Balsamic Salmon

Prep Time: 5 minutes | **Cook Time:** 8 minutes | **Serves:** 2

Oil, for spraying
2 (150g) salmon fillets
60ml balsamic vinegar
2 tablespoons honey
2 teaspoons red pepper flakes
2 teaspoons olive oil
½ teaspoon salt
¼ teaspoon freshly ground black pepper

1. Line the air fryer basket with parchment and sprinkle with oil lightly. 2. Put the salmon fillets in the air fryer basket prepared before. 3. Whisk the balsamic vinegar, honey, red pepper flakes, olive oil, salt, and black pepper in a small bowl, then brush the salmon fillets with the mixture. 4. Cook the salmon fillets at 200°C for 7 to 8 minutes until they have an internal temperature of 60°C. 5. Serve hot.
Per Serving: Calories 628; Fat 21.7g; Sodium 853mg; Carbs 23.12g; Fibre 0.2g; Sugar 22.15g; Protein 80.04g

Delicious Prawns Kebabs

Prep Time: 15 minutes | **Cook Time:** 6 minutes | **Serves:** 4

Oil, for spraying
450g medium raw prawns, peeled and deveined
4 tablespoons unsalted butter, melted
1 tablespoon Old Bay seasoning
1 tablespoon packed light brown sugar
1 teaspoon granulated garlic
1 teaspoon onion powder
½ teaspoon freshly ground black pepper

1.Line the air fryer basket with parchment and sprinkle with oil lightly. 2. Thread the prawns onto the skewers and place them in the air fryer basket prepared before. 3. Mix the butter, Old Bay, brown sugar, garlic, onion powder, and black pepper in a small bowl. Brush the sauce on the prawns. 4. Cook the prawns at 205°C for 5 to 6 minutes until pink and firm. 5. Serve hot.
Per Serving: Calories 375; Fat 10.04g; Sodium 663mg; Carbs 56.22g; Fibre 0.3g; Sugar 13.12g; Protein 16.13g

Flavourful Hot Crab Dip

Prep Time: 5 minutes | **Cook Time:** 12 minutes | **Serves:** 8

Oil, for spraying
100g cream cheese, at room temperature
60g sour cream
60g mayonnaise
200g lump crabmeat, fresh or frozen and thawed
60g shredded cheddar cheese
1 tablespoon dry Italian seasoning
1 teaspoon finely chopped fresh parsley (optional)

1. Line an air fryer-safe ramekin or casserole-style dish with parchment and sprinkle with oil lightly. 2. Mix the cream cheese, sour cream, and mayonnaise. Fold in the crabmeat, cheese, and Italian seasoning in a small bowl. Replace to the prepared ramekin. 3. Cook them at 160°C for 12 minutes. 4. Sprinkle with the parsley (if using) and serve warm.
Per Serving: Calories 154; Fat 11.57g; Sodium 274mg; Carbs 8.1g; Fibre 0.2g; Sugar 6.36g; Protein 154g

Spanish Quick Paella

Prep Time: 7 minutes | **Cook Time:** 15 minutes | **Serves:** 4

1 (250g) package frozen cooked rice, thawed
1 (150g) jar artichoke hearts, drained and chopped
60ml vegetable stock
½ teaspoon turmeric
½ teaspoon dried thyme
130g frozen cooked small prawns
100g frozen baby peas
1 tomato, diced

1. Gently stir the rice, artichoke hearts, vegetable stock, turmeric, and thyme in a suitable pan. 2. Put the pan in the air fryer, and bake the mixture for 8 to 9 minutes at 170°C until the rice is hot. 3. When cooked, transfer the dish to the serving plate, and gently stir in the prawns, peas, and tomato. Enjoy.
Per Serving: Calories 174; Fat 1.97g; Sodium 96mg; Carbs 34.74g; Fibre 5g; Sugar 9.94g; Protein 5.47g

Perfect Seafood Tacos

Prep Time: 15 minutes | **Cook Time:** 10 minutes | **Serves:** 4

455g white fish fillets, such as snapper
1 tablespoon olive oil
3 tablespoons lemon juice, divided
135g chopped red cabbage
140g salsa
70g sour cream
6 soft flour tortillas
2 avocados, peeled and chopped

1. Brush the fish with olive oil and sprinkle with 1 tablespoon of the lemon juice. Put in the air fryer basket and air-fry for 9 to 12 minutes. 2. Meanwhile, combine remaining 2 tablespoons lemon juice, cabbage, salsa, and sour cream in a medium bowl. 3. When the fish is cooked, remove from the air fryer basket and break into large pieces. 4. Let everyone assemble their own taco combining the fish, tortillas, cabbage mixture, and avocados.
Per Serving: Calories 177; Fat 3.92g; Sodium 26mg; Carbs 37.43g; Fibre 4.6g; Sugar 31.08g; Protein 2.06g

Great Herbed Salmon

Prep Time: 5 minutes | **Cook Time:** 12 minutes | **Serves:** 4

4 (150g) skinless salmon fillets
3 tablespoons honey mustard
½ teaspoon dried thyme
½ teaspoon dried basil
30g panko bread crumbs
10g crushed potato crisps
2 tablespoons olive oil

1. Put the salmon on a plate. Combine in a small bowl the mustard, thyme, and basil, and spread evenly over the salmon. 2. In another small bowl, combine the bread crumbs and potato chips and mix well. Drizzle in the olive oil and mix until combined. 3. Put the salmon in the air fryer basket and gently but firmly press the bread crumb mixture onto the top of each fillet. 4. Bake them for 9 to 12 minutes at 160°C. 5. Serve warm.
Per Serving: Calories 231; Fat 11.57g; Sodium 305 mg; Carbs 10.92g; Fibre 1g; Sugar 0.32g; Protein 20.42g

Delicious Catfish Bites

Prep Time: 15 minutes | **Cook Time:** 20 minutes | **Serves:** 4

Oil, for spraying
450g catfish fillets, cut into 5 cm pieces
240ml buttermilk
80g polenta
30g plain flour
2 teaspoons Creole seasoning
125g yellow mustard

1. Line the air fryer basket with parchment and sprinkle with oil lightly. 2. Put the catfish pieces and buttermilk in a zip-top plastic bag, then seal the bag, and refrigerate them for 10 minutes. 3. Mix in a shallow bowl together the polenta, flour, and Creole seasoning. 4. Remove the catfish pieces from the bag, and pat them dry with a paper towel. 5. Spread the mustard on all sides of the catfish, then dip them in the polenta mixture until evenly coated. 6. Put the catfish pieces in the air fryer basket prepared before, and lightly sprinkle them with oil. 7. Cook the catfish pieces at 205°C for 10 minutes; flip them carefully, spray with oil, and cook for 10 more minutes. 8. Serve warm.

Per Serving: Calories 267; Fat 6.32g; Sodium 613mg; Carbs 27.14g; Fibre 2.4g; Sugar 3.71g; Protein 24.03g

Family Favorite Thai-style Prawns Stir-fry

Prep Time: 15 minutes | **Cook Time:** 15 minutes | **Serves:** 4

200g fresh green beans
6 mini peppers, thinly sliced
2 tablespoons olive oil
455g jumbo raw prawns, peeled and deveined
120ml Thai stir-fry sauce
1 tablespoon minced garlic
315g cooked jasmine or white rice
5g shredded Thai basil

1. Toss together the green beans, peppers, and olive oil in an air fryer–safe pan. 2. Cook them at 175°C for 5 minutes. 3. Add the prawns, stir, and cook for 5 more minutes. 4. Add the stir-fry sauce and garlic, stir, and cook for 5 more minutes. 5. Serve the dish over rice with a sprinkle of Thai basil on top.

Per Serving: Calories 338; Fat 9.67g; Sodium 1063mg; Carbs 32.69g; Fibre 2.7g; Sugar 4.48g; Protein 29.65g

Delightful Crispy Fried Calamari

Prep Time: 10 minutes | **Cook Time:** 8 minutes | **Serves:** 4

Oil, for spraying
30g plain flour
2 teaspoons salt, plus more if desired
2 teaspoons freshly ground black pepper
1 large egg
450g calamari, cut into rings

1. Turn on and preheat the air fryer to 175°C. Line the air fryer basket with parchment and sprinkle with oil lightly. 2. Combine the flour, salt, and black pepper in a zip-top plastic bag and set aside. 3. In a medium bowl, whisk the egg. Add the calamari and turn to coat evenly. 4. Replace the calamari to the zip-top bag, seal, and shake well until evenly coated. 5. Put the calamari in the air fryer basket prepared before and sprinkle with oil lightly. 6. Cook the calamari for 5 minutes; flip and spray with oil, and cook for another 3 minutes. 7. Sprinkle the dish with additional salt, if desired.

Per Serving: Calories 257; Fat 14.8g; Sodium 1251mg; Carbs 7.62g; Fibre 0.5g; Sugar 0.05g; Protein 23.41g

Easy Garlic Pesto Scallops

Prep Time: 5 minutes | **Cook Time:** 5 minutes | **Serves:** 4

Oil, for spraying
60g basil pesto
3 tablespoons heavy cream
1 tablespoon olive oil
2 teaspoons minced garlic
1 teaspoon salt
½ teaspoon freshly ground black pepper
450g sea scallops

1. Line the air fryer basket with parchment and sprinkle with oil lightly. 2. In a small saucepan, Combine the pesto, heavy cream, olive oil, garlic, salt, and black pepper in a saucepan, and bring to a simmer over medium heat, stirring occasionally, cook them for 2 minutes and set aside. 3. Put the scallops in the air fryer basket prepared before. 4. Cook the scallops at 160°C for 5 minutes, flipping after 3 minutes to ensure both sides cook evenly. 5. Replace to a serving dish, pour the pesto sauce over the top.
Per Serving: Calories 237; Fat 14.36g; Sodium 686mg; Carbs 1.01g; Fibre 0.1g; Sugar 0.33g; Protein 26.37g

Irresistible Chili-Lime Tilapia

Prep Time: 5 minutes | **Cook Time:** 8 minutes | **Serves:** 4

½ teaspoon salt
½ teaspoon freshly ground black pepper
¼ teaspoon garlic powder
¼ teaspoon chili powder
¼ teaspoon smoked paprika
4 (100g) tilapia fillets
2 tablespoons freshly squeezed lime juice

1. Turn on and preheat the air fryer to 205°C. Line the air fryer basket with parchment paper. 2. Mix in a small bowl together the salt, pepper, garlic powder, chili powder, and paprika. 3. Put the fish fillets in a shallow bowl. Pour the lime juice over the fillets and then sprinkle it with the spice blend, making sure to coat all sides well. 4. Put the fish in the air fryer basket in a single layer, leaving space between each fillet. Cook the fish for 4 minutes; turn the fish over and cook for an another 4 to 5 minutes until crispy. 5. Serve immediately.
Per Serving: Calories 116; Fat 2.03g; Sodium 356mg; Carbs 1.14g; Fibre 0.2 g; Sugar 0.16g; Protein 23.43g

Easy and Delicious Coriander Butter Baked Mahi Mahi

Prep Time: 5 minutes | **Cook Time:** 15 minutes | **Serves:** 4

2 tablespoons butter, melted
2 tablespoons chopped fresh coriander
2 garlic cloves, minced
½ teaspoon salt
¼ teaspoon freshly ground black pepper
¼ teaspoon chili powder
4 (100g) boneless, skinless mahi-mahi fillets

1. Turn on and preheat the air fryer to 190°C. 2. Mix the butter, coriander, garlic, salt, pepper, and chili powder in a small bowl. 3. Put the mahi-mahi fillets on a large plate. Spread the butter mixture over the top of the fillets. 4. Put a piece of parchment paper in the air fryer basket. Put the fish in a single layer in the air fryer basket. Cook them for 6 minutes; turn them over and cook for an another 6 to 7 minutes until flaky.
Per Serving: Calories 103; Fat 7.41g; Sodium 418mg; Carbs 6.62g; Fibre 0.6g; Sugar 1.56g; Protein 2.83g

Delicate Steamed Tuna

Prep Time: 10 minutes | **Cook Time:** 10 minutes | **Serves:** 4

4 small tuna steaks
2 tablespoons low-sodium soy sauce
2 teaspoons sesame oil
2 teaspoons rice wine vinegar
1 teaspoon grated fresh ginger
⅛ teaspoon pepper
1 stalk lemongrass, bent in half
3 tablespoons lemon juice

1. Put the tuna steaks on a plate. 2. Combine the soy sauce, sesame oil, rice wine vinegar, and ginger in a small bowl. Pour this mixture over the tuna and marinate for 10 minutes. Rub the soy sauce mixture gently into both sides of the tuna, and sprinkle with the pepper. 3. Put the lemongrass on the air fryer basket and put on the top the steaks. Put the lemon juice and 1 tablespoon water in the pan below the air fryer basket. 4. Steam the fish for 8 to 10 minutes at 200°C. 5. When cooked, discard the lemongrass and serve the tuna.
Per Serving: Calories 307; Fat 15.99 g; Sodium 810mg; Carbs 2.92g; Fibre 0.1g; Sugar 0.41g; Protein 810g

Easy Tuna Veggie Stir-Fry

Prep Time: 15 minutes | **Cook Time:** 10 minutes | **Serves:** 4

1 tablespoon olive oil
1 red pepper, chopped
100g green beans, cut into 5 cm pieces
1 onion, sliced
2 cloves garlic, sliced
2 tablespoons low-sodium soy sauce
1 tablespoon honey
225g fresh tuna, cubed

1. Combine the olive oil, pepper, green beans, onion, and garlic in a suitable metal bowl. 2. Cook the bean mixture in the air fryer for 4 to 6 minutes until crisp and tender, stirring once; stir in the soy sauce, honey, and tuna, and cook them for 4 to 6 minutes at 195°C, stirring once, until crisp and tender. 3. Cook them for another 3 to 6 minutes, stirring once. Tuna can be served rare or medium-rare.
Per Serving: Calories 115; Fat 4.18g; Sodium 398mg; Carbs 8.07g; Fibre 1g; Sugar 5.35g; Protein 12.44g

Quick Scallops and Spring Veggies

Prep Time: 10 minutes | **Cook Time:** 8 minutes | **Serves:** 4

225g asparagus, ends trimmed, cut into 5 cm pieces
100g sugar snap peas
445g sea scallops
1 tablespoon lemon juice
2 teaspoons olive oil
½ teaspoon dried thyme
Pinch salt
Freshly ground black pepper

1. Put the asparagus and sugar snap peas in the air fryer basket. Cook them for 2 to 3 minutes. 2. Meanwhile, check the scallops for a small muscle attached to the side, and pull it off and discard. 3. Toss in a medium bowl the scallops with the lemon juice, olive oil, thyme, salt, and pepper. Put into the air fryer basket on top of the vegetables. 4. Steam them for 5 to 7 minutes at 205°C, tossing them once during cooking time, until the scallops are just firm when tested with your finger and are opaque in the centre, and the vegetables are tender.
Per Serving: Calories 204; Fat 8.13g; Sodium 684mg; Carbs 5.45g; Fibre 2.5g; Sugar 1.17g; Protein 28.3g

Popular Fried Garlic Prawns

Prep Time: 15 minutes | **Cook Time:** 10 minutes | **Serves:** 3

For Prawns
Oil, for spraying
450g medium raw prawns, peeled and deveined
6 tablespoons unsalted butter, melted
110g panko bread crumbs
2 tablespoons granulated garlic
1 teaspoon salt
½ teaspoon freshly ground black pepper

For Garlic Butter Sauce
115g unsalted butter
2 teaspoons granulated garlic
¾ teaspoon salt (omit if using salted butter)

1. Turn on and preheat the air fryer to 205°C. Line the air fryer basket with parchment and sprinkle with oil lightly. 2. Put the prawns and melted butter in a zip-top plastic bag, seal the bag, and shake until evenly coated. 3. Mix the bread crumbs, garlic, salt, and black pepper in a medium bowl. 4. Add the prawns to the panko mixture and toss until evenly coated. Shake off any excess coating. 5. Put the prawns in the air fryer basket prepared before and sprinkle with oil lightly. 6. Cook the prawns for 8 to 10 minutes until golden brown and crispy, flipping and spraying them with oil after 4 to 5 minutes of cooking time. 7. Combine the butter, garlic, and salt in a microwave-safe bowl, and microwave them on 50% power for 30 to 60 seconds, stirring every 15 seconds. 8. Serve the prawns with the garlic butter sauce on the side for dipping.
Per Serving: Calories 490; Fat 39.46g; Sodium 2294mg; Carbs 9.89g; Fibre 0.6g; Sugar 0.74g; Protein 24.29g

Easy French Mussels

Prep Time: 5 minutes | **Cook Time:** 8 minutes | **Serves:** 4

Oil, for spraying
455g blue mussels
1 tablespoon unsalted butter
2 teaspoons minced garlic
1 teaspoon dried chives
1 teaspoon dried basil
1 teaspoon dried parsley
240ml water
Lemon wedges, for garnish

1. Line the air fryer basket with parchment and sprinkle with oil lightly. 2. Run the mussels under cold water and, using a clean scrub brush, remove any debris. Lightly tap any open shells and toss those that don't close. 3. Combine the butter, garlic, chives, basil, parsley, and water in a microwave-safe bowl. Microwave them on high for 30 to 40 seconds; stir to combine and reserve half of the sauce in a small bowl. 4. Add the mussels to the remaining sauce and toss to coat. 5. Put the mussels in the air fryer basket prepared before. 6. Cook the mussels at 200°C for 4 minutes, stir, and cook for another 4 minutes Discard any that do not open. 7. Replace to a serving bowl, drizzle with the reserved sauce, and garnish with lemon wedges.
Per Serving: Calories 130; Fat 5.64g; Sodium 327mg; Carbs 5.59g; Fibre 0.1g; Sugar 0.33g; Protein 13.8g

Great Cod with Creamy Mustard Sauce

Prep Time: 10 minutes | **Cook Time:** 5 minutes | **Serves:** 4

For Fish
Oil, for spraying
450g cod fillets
2 tablespoons olive oil
1 tablespoon lemon juice
1 teaspoon salt
½ teaspoon freshly ground black pepper

For Mustard Sauce
120g heavy cream
3 tablespoons Dijon mustard
1 tablespoon unsalted butter
1 teaspoon salt

1. Line the air fryer basket with parchment and sprinkle with oil lightly. 2. Rub the cod with the olive oil and lemon juice. Season with the salt and black pepper. 3. Put the cod fillets in the air fryer basket prepared before. 4. Cook the cod fillets at 175°C for 5 minutes. Turn the temperature to 205°C and cook for 5 more minutes, until they have an internal temperature of 60°C.5. Add the heavy cream, mustard, butter, and salt to the saucepan, and bring to a simmer over low heat; then cook them for 3 to 4 minutes until the sauce starts to thicken.. 6. Replace the cod fillets to a serving plate, and drizzle with the mustard sauce. Enjoy.
Per Serving: Calories 476; Fat 36.18g; Sodium 1855mg; Carbs 11.81g; Fibre 7.5g; Sugar 1.53g; Protein 26.99g

Crisp Flounder au Gratin

Prep Time: 5 minutes | **Cook Time:** 12 minutes | **Serves:** 4

4 (150g) flounder fillets
4 tablespoons unsalted butter, melted, divided
30g whole-wheat panko bread crumbs
25g grated Parmesan cheese
½ teaspoon salt
½ teaspoon dried oregano
½ teaspoon dried basil
¼ teaspoon freshly ground black pepper
1 lemon, quartered
1 tablespoon chopped fresh parsley

1. Turn on and preheat the air fryer to 190°C. 2. Pat dry the fish fillets and brush them with 2 tablespoons of butter, making sure to coat them on all sides. 3. Mix in a small bowl together the remaining 2 tablespoons of butter, bread crumbs, Parmesan cheese, salt, oregano, basil, and pepper until it becomes a moist but crumbly mixture. 4. Dredge the fish in the bread crumb mixture, making sure to press the crumbs onto the fish, until well coated. Put the fillets in the air fryer basket and cook for 5 minutes. Turn and cook them for an another 5 to 7 minutes. 5. Serve with lemon wedges and a sprinkle of fresh parsley.
Per Serving: Calories 377; Fat 24.94g; Sodium 825mg; Carbs 15.8g; Fibre 5.6g; Sugar 1.02g; Protein 22.91g

Lemon-Herb Tuna Steaks

Prep Time: 20 minutes | **Cook Time:** 7 minutes | **Serves:** 4

½ tablespoon extra-virgin olive oil
1 garlic clove, minced
¼ teaspoon salt
¼ teaspoon chili powder
1 tablespoon plus 1 teaspoon freshly squeezed lemon juice
1 tablespoon chopped fresh coriander
4 (100g) tuna steaks, about 2.5cm thick
1 lemon, thinly sliced

1. In a wide, shallow bowl, mix together the olive oil, garlic, salt, chili powder, lemon juice, and coriander. Put the tuna steaks in the mixture, turning the steaks to coat them on all sides. Cover loosely and set aside to marinate for 20 minutes. 2. Turn on and preheat the air fryer to 195°C. 3. Put a piece of parchment paper in the air fryer basket. Remove the tuna steaks from the marinade and place them in the air fryer basket in one layer. Discard any remaining marinade. Cook for 7 minutes. Remove the air fryer basket from the air fryer and let stand for 5 minutes. 4. Put the tuna steaks on plates, and top them the lemon slices, then enjoy.
Per Serving: Calories 135; Fat 1.37g; Sodium 217mg; Carbs 1.26g; Fibre 0.36g; Sugar 13.12g; Protein 27.8g

Zesty Lemon-Caper Salmon Burgers

Prep Time: 15 minutes | **Cook Time:** 12 minutes | **Serves:** 4

455g boneless, skinless salmon fillet
1 spring onion, both white and green parts, diced
2 tablespoons clean mayonnaise, plus more for serving
1 egg
1 teaspoon capers, drained
½ teaspoon salt
½ teaspoon freshly ground black pepper
¼ teaspoon paprika
Zest of 1 lemon
30g whole-wheat bread crumbs
4 whole-wheat buns, toasted
4 teaspoons whole-grain mustard
4 lettuce leaves
1 small tomato, sliced

1. Turn on and preheat the air fryer to 205°C. 2. Cut the salmon in half. Cut one half into chunks and place them into a food processor. Add the spring onion, mayonnaise, egg, capers, salt, pepper, paprika, and lemon zest and pulse until the salmon is pureed. 3. Dice the remaining half of salmon into ½ cm pieces. 4. Combine the salmon pieces, pureed salmon, and bread crumbs in a large bowl. 5. Form the mixture into 4 patties and place them in the air fryer basket. Cook for 5 minutes. Turn over the patties and continue cooking for an another 5 to 7 minutes. 6. Serve the salmon burgers on the whole-wheat buns with a teaspoon of mustard, more mayonnaise, lettuce, and a slice of tomato.
Per Serving: Calories 293; Fat 11.58g; Sodium 742mg; Carbs 32.74g; Fibre 2.9g; Sugar 7g; Protein 14.65g

Efficient Cod Piccata with Roasted Potatoes

Prep Time: 15 minutes | **Cook Time:** 12 minutes | **Serves:** 4

4 (100g) cod fillets
1 tablespoon unsalted butter
2 teaspoons capers, drained
1 garlic clove, minced
2 tablespoons freshly squeezed lemon juice
225g asparagus, trimmed
2 large potatoes, cubed
1 tablespoon extra-virgin olive oil
¼ teaspoon salt
¼ teaspoon garlic powder
¼ teaspoon freshly ground black pepper

1. Turn on and preheat the air fryer to 195°C. 2. Put the cod fillets on a large piece of aluminum foil. Add the butter, capers, garlic, and lemon juice over the cod and wrap up the foil to enclose the fish in a pouch. 3. Toss in a large bowl together the asparagus, potatoes, olive oil, salt, garlic powder, and pepper. 4. Replace the potatoes and asparagus to the air fryer basket and cook for 4 minutes. Shake or stir the air fryer basket and carefully place the foil packet of fish on top of the vegetables. Continue cooking for 8 minutes. 5. Let the dish stand for 5 minutes before serving.
Per Serving: Calories 436; Fat 19.03g; Sodium 707mg; Carbs 43.31g; Fibre 10.7g; Sugar 3.41g; Protein 24.88g

Fresh Garlic-Dill Salmon with Tomatoes & Green Beans

Prep Time: 5 minutes | **Cook Time:** 15 minutes | **Serves:** 4

4 tablespoons unsalted butter
4 garlic cloves, minced
10g chopped fresh dill
½ teaspoon salt
½ teaspoon freshly ground black pepper
4 (100g) wild-caught salmon fillets, skin removed
1 lemon, thinly sliced
455g green beans, trimmed
150g halved cherry tomatoes

1. Turn on and preheat the air fryer to 200°C. Line the air fryer basket with parchment paper. 2. Mix in a small bowl together the butter, garlic, dill, salt, and pepper. 3. Put the salmon fillets on a large plate and spread the butter mixture over them. 4. Put the salmon in the air fryer basket in a single layer. Put about three-quarters of the lemon slices on top of the fillets. Put the green beans and tomatoes around the fillets. 5. Cook for 12 to 15 minutes. 6. Serve with the remaining lemon slices.
Per Serving: Calories 515; Fat 22.86g; Sodium 1257mg; Carbs 12.4g; Fibre 3g; Sugar 5.85g; Protein 67.52 g

Satisfying Parmesan Perch

Prep Time: 5 minutes | **Cook Time:** 10 minutes | **Serves:** 5

½ teaspoon salt
¼ teaspoon paprika
¼ teaspoon freshly ground black pepper
1 tablespoon chopped fresh dill
25g grated Parmesan cheese
2 tablespoons whole-wheat bread crumbs
4 (100g) ocean perch fillets
Extra-virgin olive oil, in a spray bottle, for greasing
1 lemon, quartered

1. Turn on and preheat the air fryer to 205°C. Line the air fryer basket with parchment paper. 2. Combine the salt, paprika, pepper, dill, Parmesan cheese, and bread crumbs in a shallow bowl. 3. Dip the fillets in the Parmesan mixture, turning them to coat on all sides. 4. Put the perch fillets in a single layer in the air fryer basket, and spray the fillets with olive oil. Cook them for 7 to 9 minutes until the crust is golden. 5. Serve the perch fillets with the lemon wedges.
Per Serving: Calories 111; Fat 3.25g; Sodium 612mg; Carbs 4.19g; Fibre 0.5g; Sugar 0.43g; Protein 15.95g

Perfect Haddock Fish Fingers

Prep Time: 10 minutes | **Cook Time:** 10 minutes | **Serves:** 4

30g whole-wheat flour
¼ teaspoon salt
¼ teaspoon freshly ground black pepper
¼ teaspoon smoked paprika
¼ teaspoon dried oregano
1 egg
1 teaspoon water
4 (100g) haddock fillets
1 lemon, thinly sliced (optional)
Malt vinegar, for serving (optional)
Ketchup, for serving (optional)
Tartar sauce, for serving (optional)

1. Turn on and preheat the air fryer to 205°C. Line the air fryer with parchment paper. 2. In a wide, shallow bowl, mix together the flour, salt, pepper, paprika, and oregano. 3. In a separate wide shallow bowl, whisk together the egg and water. 4. Pat dry the haddock and cut each fillet into 4 strips. Dip each strip into the egg first, letting any excess drip off, and then in the flour mixture until coated on all sides. 5. Put the fish in the air fryer basket in a single layer and cook for 4 minutes. Turn over the fish and continue cooking for an another 4 to 5 minutes until crisp. 6. If desired, serve with sliced lemon, vinegar, ketchup, or tartar sauce.
Per Serving: Calories 204; Fat 3.52g; Sodium 853mg; Carbs 6.71g; Fibre 1g; Sugar 0.52g; Protein 34.82g

Juicy Teriyaki Salmon

Prep Time: 6 minutes | **Cook Time:** 12 minutes | **Serves:** 4

4 (150g) salmon fillets
120ml soy sauce
55g light brown sugar
2 teaspoons rice vinegar
1 teaspoon minced garlic
¼ teaspoon ground ginger
2 teaspoons olive oil
½ teaspoon salt
¼ teaspoon freshly ground black pepper
Oil, for spraying

1. Put the salmon the fillets in a small pan with skin-side up. 2. Whisk the soy sauce, brown sugar, rice vinegar, garlic, ginger, olive oil, salt, and black pepper in a small bowl. 3. Pour the mixture over the salmon fillets and marinate them for 30 minutes. 4. Line the air fryer basket with parchment and sprinkle with oil lightly. Put the salmon in the air fryer basket prepared before, skin-side down. 5. Cook the salmon fillets at 205°C for 6 minutes, brush the salmon with more marinade, and cook for 6 more minutes.
Per Serving: Calories 607; Fat 24.4g; Sodium 975mg; Carbs 9.28g; Fibre 0.7g; Sugar 6.44g; Protein 82.27g

Distinct Cajun Prawns

Prep Time: 15 minutes | **Cook Time:** 9 minutes | **Serves:** 4

Oil, for spraying
450g jumbo raw prawns, peeled and deveined
1 tablespoon Cajun seasoning
150g cooked kielbasa, cut into thick slices
½ medium courgette, cut into ½ cm-thick slices
½ medium yellow squash, cut into ½ cm-thick slices
1 green pepper, seeded and cut into 2.5 cm pieces
2 tablespoons olive oil
½ teaspoon salt

1. Turn on and preheat the air fryer to 205°C. Line the air fryer basket with parchment and sprinkle with oil lightly. 2. Toss the prawns and Cajun seasoning in a large bowl; mix in the kielbasa, courgette, squash, pepper, olive oil, and salt. 3. Replace the mixture to the air fryer basket prepared before. 4. Cook the prawns for 9 minutes, shaking the basket and stirring the prawns every 3 minutes. . 5. Serve hot.
Per Serving: Calories 291; Fat 16.93g; Sodium 1945mg; Carbs 4.06g; Fibre 0.5g; Sugar 0.83g; Protein 29.1g

Simple Snapper Scampi

Prep Time: 5 minutes | **Cook Time:** 10 minutes | **Serves:** 4

4 (150g) skinless snapper
1 tablespoon olive oil
3 tablespoons lemon juice, divided
½ teaspoon dried basil
Pinch salt
Freshly ground black pepper
2 tablespoons butter
2 cloves garlic, minced

1. Rub the fish fillets with olive oil and 1 tablespoon of the lemon juice. Sprinkle with the basil, salt, and pepper, and place in the air fryer basket. 2. Grill the fish for 7 to 8 minutes at 195°C. Remove the fish from the air fryer basket and put on a serving plate. Cover to keep warm. 3. In a 15 cm x 5 cm pan, combine the butter, remaining 2 tablespoons lemon juice, and garlic. Cook in the air fryer for 1 to 2 minutes. 4. Pour this mixture over the fish and serve.
Per Serving: Calories 305; Fat 12.11g; Sodium 853mg; Carbs 1.71g; Fibre 0.2g; Sugar 0.31g; Protein 44.99g

Delicate Crab Ratatouille

Prep Time: 15 minutes | **Cook Time:** 11 minutes | **Serves:** 4

125g peeled, cubed aubergine
1 onion, chopped
1 red pepper, chopped
2 large tomatoes, chopped
1 tablespoon olive oil
½ teaspoon dried thyme
½ teaspoon dried basil
Pinch salt
Freshly ground black pepper
330g cooked crabmeat, picked over

1. Combine the aubergine, onion, pepper, tomatoes, olive oil, thyme, and basil in a 15 cm metal bowl, then sprinkle them with salt and pepper. 2. Roast them for 9 minutes at 205°C, then remove the bowl from the air fryer and stir. 3. Add the crabmeat and roast for 2 to 5 minutes until the ratatouille is bubbling and the vegetables are tender. 4. Serve and enjoy.
Per Serving: Calories 320; Fat 11. 27g; Sodium 853mg; Carbs 49.52g; Fibre 3.4g; Sugar 13.12g; Protein 5.85g

Chapter 4 Poultry Recipes

Cajun Pepper & Chicken Kebabs

Prep Time: 20 minutes| **Cook Time:** 20 minutes| **Serves:** 6

Olive oil
775g boneless, skinless chicken breasts, cut into bite-sized chunks
1½ tablespoons Cajun seasoning, divided
1 medium red pepper, cut into big chunks
1 medium green pepper, cut into big chunks
1 medium onion, cut into big chunks

1. Spray an air fryer basket lightly with olive oil. 2. Toss the chicken with 1 tablespoon of Cajun seasoning in a large bowl, and spray with olive oil to coat. 3. In a separate, large bowl, toss the peppers and onion with the remaining ½ tablespoon of Cajun seasoning, and spray with olive oil to coat. 4. If using wooden skewers, soak them in water for at least 30 minutes before using. 5. Thread the chicken chunks and vegetables onto the skewers, alternating with chicken, then vegetable. 6. Transfer the skewers to the air fryer basket in a single layer. You may need to cook them in batches. 7. Air fry at 175°C for 10 minutes. Flip the skewers over and lightly spray with olive oil. Air fry until the chicken has an internal temperature of at least 75°C, another 5 to 10 minutes.
Per Serving: Calories 152; Fat 4.24 g; Sodium 352 mg; Carbs 4.86 g; Fibre 1.1 g; Sugar 2.22 g; Protein 23.69 g

Pineapple Chicken Kebabs

Prep Time: 15 minutes, plus 1 to 2 hours to marinate| **Cook Time:** 20 minutes| **Serves:** 6

Olive oil
3 tablespoons soy sauce
1 (375g) can pineapple chunks, 2 tablespoons of the juice reserved
1 tablespoon sesame oil
¼ teaspoon ground ginger
¼ teaspoon garlic powder
775g boneless, skinless chicken breasts, cut into 2.5 cm chunks
2 large peppers

1. Spray an air fryer basket lightly with olive oil. Cut the peppers into 2.5 cm chunks. 2.Mix together the soy sauce, the reserved pineapple juice, sesame oil, ginger, and garlic powder in a large bowl. Add the chicken, peppers, and pineapple chunks and toss to coat. 3.Cover the bowl and then refrigerate it for at least 1 hour and up to 2 hours. 4.If using wooden skewers, soak the skewers in water for at least 30 minutes. 5.Thread the chicken, peppers, and pineapple onto the skewers, alternating with chicken, vegetable, and fruit. Place the skewers in the air fryer basket in a single layer. Lightly spray the skewers with olive oil. Cook the kebabs in batches as needed. 6.Air fry at 175°C for 10 minutes. Turn the skewers over, lightly spray with olive oil, and cook until the chicken is nicely browned and the veggies are starting to char on the edges, for an additional 5 to 10 minutes.
Per Serving: Calories 235; Fat 7.52 g; Sodium 173 mg; Carbs 14.69 g; Fibre 1 g; Sugar 12.55 g; Protein 26.71 g

Lemon Pepper Chicken Drumsticks

Prep Time: 5 minutes| **Cook Time:** 25 minutes| **Serves:** 2

2 teaspoons baking powder
½ teaspoon garlic powder
8 chicken drumsticks
4 tablespoons salted butter, melted
1 tablespoon lemon pepper seasoning

1. Sprinkle baking powder and garlic powder over drumsticks and rub into chicken skin. Place drumsticks into the air fryer basket. 2. Adjust the temperature setting to 190°C and set the timer for 25 minutes. 3. Use tongs to turn drumsticks halfway through the cooking time. 4. When skin is golden and the internal temperature is at least 75°C, remove from air fryer. 5. In a large bowl, mix butter and lemon pepper seasoning. Add drumsticks to the bowl and toss until coated. Serve warm.
Per Serving (8 drumsticks): Calories 495; Fat 31.68 g; Sodium 419 mg; Carbs 2.72 g; Fibre 0.3 g; Sugar 0.16 g; Protein 47.34 g

Stuffed Chicken Breast

Prep Time: 15 minutes| **Cook Time:** 25 minutes| **Serves:** 4

2 (150g) boneless, skinless chicken breasts
¼ medium white onion, peeled and cut into slices
1 medium green pepper, seeded and sliced
1 tablespoon coconut oil
2 teaspoons chili powder
1 teaspoon ground cumin
½ teaspoon garlic powder

1. Slice each chicken breast completely in half lengthwise into two even pieces. Using a meat tenderizer, pound out the chicken until it's about ½ cm thickness. 2. Lay each slice of chicken out and place three slices of onion and four slices of green pepper on the end closest to you. Begin rolling the peppers and onions tightly into the chicken. Secure the roll with either toothpicks or a couple pieces of butcher's twine. 3. Drizzle coconut oil over chicken. Sprinkle each side with chili powder, cumin, and garlic powder. Place the rolls evenly into the air fryer basket. 4. Adjust the temperature to 175°C and set the timer for 25 minutes. 5. Serve warm.
Per Serving: Calories 117; Fat 7.68 g; Sodium 68 mg; Carbs 2.9 g; Fibre 0.8 g; Sugar 0.98 g; Protein 9.51 g

Mozzarella Chicken Pizza Crust

Prep Time: 10 minutes| **Cook Time:** 25 minutes| **Serves:** 4

445g chicken thigh mince
25g grated Parmesan cheese
55g shredded mozzarella

1. Mix the chicken thigh meat, Parmesan cheese, and shredded mozzarella together in a large bowl. Separate into four even parts. 2. Cut out four (15 cm) circles of parchment paper and press each portion of the chicken-cheese mixture out onto one of the circles. Then place the circles into the air fryer basket, working in batches as needed. 3. Adjust the temperature setting to 190°C and set the timer for 25 minutes. 4. Flip the crust halfway through the cooking time. 5. Once fully cooked, you may top it with cheese and your favorite toppings and cook for 5 additional minutes. Or, you may place crust into the refrigerator or freezer and top when ready to eat.
Per Serving: Calories 183; Fat 6.41 g; Sodium 325 mg; Carbs 1.36 g; Fibre 0.3 g; Sugar 0.21 g; Protein 28.55 g

Crusted Chicken

Prep Time: 15 minutes| **Cook Time:** 25 minutes| **Serves:** 4

30g slivered almonds
2 (150g) boneless, skinless chicken breasts
2 tablespoons full-fat mayonnaise
1 tablespoon Dijon mustard

1. Pulse the almonds with a food processor or chop until finely chopped. Place almonds evenly on a plate and set aside. 2. Completely slice each chicken breast in half lengthwise. 3. Mix the mayonnaise and mustard in a small bowl and then coat chicken with the mixture. 4. Lay each piece of chicken in the chopped almonds to fully coat. Carefully move the pieces into the air fryer basket. 5. Adjust the temperature setting to 175°C and set the timer for 25 minutes. 6. Chicken will be cooked when it has reached an internal temperature of 75°C or more. Serve warm.
Per Serving: Calories 103; Fat 7.1 g; Sodium 130 mg; Carbs 0.24 g; Fibre 0.2 g; Sugar 0.04 g; Protein 9.06 g

Simple Chicken Fajitas

Prep Time: 10 minutes| **Cook Time:** 15 minutes| **Serves:** 2

250g boneless, skinless chicken breast, sliced into ½ cm strips
2 tablespoons coconut oil, melted
1 tablespoon chili powder
½ teaspoon cumin
½ teaspoon paprika
½ teaspoon garlic powder
¼ medium onion, peeled and sliced
½ medium green pepper, seeded and sliced
½ medium red pepper, seeded and sliced

1. Add chicken and coconut oil into a large bowl and sprinkle with chili powder, cumin, paprika, and garlic powder. Toss chicken until well coated with seasoning. Place chicken into the air fryer basket. 2. Adjust the temperature setting to 175°C and set the timer for 15 minutes. 3. Add onion and peppers into the fryer basket when the timer has 7 minutes remaining. 4. Toss the chicken two or three times during cooking. Vegetables should be tender and chicken fully cooked to at least 75°C internal temperature when finished. Serve warm.
Per Serving: Calories 388; Fat 27.53 g; Sodium 421 mg; Carbs 5.24 g; Fibre 2.2 g; Sugar 1.61 g; Protein 30.81 g

"Fried" Chicken

Prep Time: 15 minutes| **Cook Time:** 25 minutes| **Serves:** 4

2 (150g) boneless, skinless chicken breasts
2 tablespoons hot sauce
1 tablespoon chili powder
½ teaspoon cumin
¼ teaspoon onion powder
¼ teaspoon ground black pepper
50g ground parmesan

1. Slice both the chicken breast in half lengthwise. Place the chicken into a large bowl and coat with hot sauce. 2. Mix chili powder, cumin, onion powder, and pepper in a small bowl. Sprinkle over chicken. 3. Place the grated parmesan into a large bowl and dip each piece of chicken into the bowl, coating as much as possible. Place chicken into the air fryer basket. 4. Adjust the temperature to 175°C and set the timer for 25 minutes. 5. Halfway through the cooking time, carefully flip the chicken. 6. When done, internal temperature will be at least 75°C and parmesan coating will be dark golden brown. Serve warm.
Per Serving: Calories 114; Fat 5.87 g; Sodium 156 mg; Carbs 2.11 g; Fibre 1 g; Sugar 0.66 g; Protein 13.03 g

Creamy Chicken Corden Bleu Casserole

Prep Time: 15 minutes| **Cook Time:** 15 minutes| **Serves:** 4

480g cubed cooked chicken thigh meat
70g cubed cooked ham
50g Swiss cheese, cubed
100g full-fat cream cheese, softened
1 tablespoon heavy cream
2 tablespoons unsalted butter, melted
2 teaspoons Dijon mustard
25g grated parmesan

1. Place chicken and ham into a 15 cm round baking pan and toss so meat is evenly mixed. Sprinkle cheese cubes on top of meat. 2. Mix cream cheese, heavy cream, butter, and Dijon mustard in a large bowl and then pour them over the meat and cheese. Top with parmesan. Place pan into the air fryer basket. 3. Adjust the temperature setting to 175°C and set the timer for 15 minutes. 4. The casserole will be browned and bubbling when done. Serve warm.
Per Serving: Calories 357; Fat 25.18 g; Sodium 433 mg; Carbs 3.49 g; Fibre 0.1 g; Sugar 2.14 g; Protein 27.97 g

Cheddar Jalapeño Popper Hasselback Chicken

Prep Time: 20 minutes| **Cook Time:** 20 minutes| **Serves:** 2

4 slices bacon, cooked and crumbled
50g full-fat cream cheese, softened
50g shredded sharp Cheddar cheese, divided
20g sliced pickled jalapeños
2 (150g) boneless, skinless chicken breasts

1. In a medium bowl, place cooked bacon, then fold in cream cheese, half of the Cheddar, and the jalapeño slices. 2. Use a sharp knife to make slits in each of the chicken breasts about ¾ of the way across the chicken, being careful not to cut all the way through. Depending on the size of the chicken breast, you'll likely have 6–8 slits per breast. 3. Transfer the cheese mixture to the slits of the chicken with a spoon. Sprinkle the remaining shredded cheese over chicken breasts and place into the air fryer basket. 4. Adjust the temperature to 175°C and set the timer for 20 minutes. 6. Serve warm.
Per Serving: Calories 426; Fat 30.37 g; Sodium 730 mg; Carbs 2.98 g; Fibre 0 g; Sugar 1.75 g; Protein 33.68 g

Cajun Thyme Chicken Tenders

Prep Time: 10 minutes| **Cook Time:** 17 minutes| **Serves:** 4

2 teaspoons paprika
1 teaspoon chili powder
½ teaspoon garlic powder
½ teaspoon dried thyme
¼ teaspoon onion powder
⅛ teaspoon ground cayenne pepper
2 tablespoons coconut oil
445g boneless, skinless chicken mini fillets
60ml full-fat ranch dressing

1. Combine all the spices in a suitable bowl. 2. Drizzle oil over chicken tenders and then generously coat each tender in the spice mixture. Place tenders into the air fryer basket. 3. Adjust the temperature setting to 190°C and set the timer for 17 minutes. 4. Tenders will be 75°C internally when fully cooked. Serve with ranch dressing for dipping.
Per Serving: Calories 209; Fat 10.38 g; Sodium 231 mg; Carbs 5.24 g; Fibre 0.7 g; Sugar 1.01 g; Protein 23.46 g

Chicken-Avocado Enchiladas

Prep Time: 20 minutes| **Cook Time:** 10 minutes| **Serves:** 4

360g shredded cooked chicken
75g enchilada sauce, divided
220g medium-sliced deli chicken
120g shredded medium Cheddar cheese
60g shredded Monterey jack cheese
115g full-fat sour cream
1 medium avocado, peeled, pitted, and sliced

1. In a large bowl, mix shredded chicken and half of the enchilada sauce. Lay slices of deli chicken on a work surface and spoon 2 tablespoons shredded chicken mixture onto each slice. 2. Sprinkle 2 tablespoons of Cheddar onto each roll. Gently roll closed. 3. In a 15 cm x 5 cm round baking dish, place each roll, seam side down. Pour the remaining sauce over rolls and then top with Monterey jack. Place dish into the air fryer basket. 4. Adjust the temperature setting to 185°C and set the timer for 10 minutes. 5. Enchiladas will be golden on top and bubbling when cooked. Serve with sour cream and avocado slices, as you like.
Per Serving: Calories 447; Fat 28.46 g; Sodium 1051 mg; Carbs 11.78 g; Fibre 3.6 g; Sugar 1.51 g; Protein 37.04 g

Mayo Chicken

Prep Time: 10 minutes| **Cook Time:** 25 minutes| **Serves:** 4

2 (150g) boneless, skinless chicken breasts
½ teaspoon garlic powder
¼ teaspoon dried oregano
½ teaspoon dried parsley
4 tablespoons full-fat mayonnaise, divided
110g shredded mozzarella cheese, divided
50g grated Parmesan cheese, divided
225g low-carb, no-sugar-added pasta sauce

1. Slice both the chicken breasts in half lengthwise and pound out to 2 cm thickness. Sprinkle with garlic powder, dried oregano, and dried parsley. 2. Spread 1 tablespoon mayonnaise on top of each piece of chicken, then sprinkle 30 g mozzarella on each piece. Sprinkle the parmesan on top of mozzarella. 4. Pour sauce into 15 cm round baking pan and place chicken on top. Place pan into the air fryer basket. 5. Adjust the temperature to 160°C and set the timer for 25 minutes. 6. Cheese will be browned and internal temperature of the chicken will be at least 75°C when fully cooked. Serve warm.
Per Serving: Calories 296; Fat 14.15 g; Sodium 599 mg; Carbs 19.52 g; Fibre 0.8 g; Sugar 13.2 g; Protein 24.1 g

Pepperoni and Chicken Pizza Bake

Prep Time: 10 minutes| **Cook Time:** 15 minutes| **Serves:** 4

280g cubed cooked chicken
20 slices pepperoni
225g low-carb, sugar-free pizza sauce
110g shredded mozzarella cheese
25g grated Parmesan cheese

1. In a 15 cm x 5 cm round baking dish add chicken, pepperoni, and pizza sauce. Stir so meat is completely covered with sauce. 2. Top with mozzarella and grated Parmesan. Place dish into the air fryer basket. 3. Adjust the temperature setting to 190°C and set the timer for 15 minutes. 4. Dish will be brown and bubbling when cooked. Serve immediately.
Per Serving: Calories 343; Fat 15.67 g; Sodium 568 mg; Carbs 18.3 g; Fibre 0.7 g; Sugar 13.18 g; Protein 32.76 g

Teriyaki Chicken Wings

Prep Time: 1 hour| **Cook Time:** 25 minutes| **Serves:** 4

900g chicken wings
120ml sugar-free teriyaki sauce
2 teaspoons minced garlic
¼ teaspoon ground ginger
2 teaspoons baking powder

1. Place all ingredients except baking powder into a large bowl or bag and let marinade for 1 hour in the refrigerator. 2. Place wings into the air fryer basket and sprinkle with baking powder. Gently rub into wings. 3. Adjust the temperature ssetting to 205°C and set the timer for 25 minutes. 4. Toss the basket two or three times during cooking. 5. Wings should be crispy and cooked to at least 75°C internally when done. Serve immediately.
Per Serving: Calories 292; Fat 8.05 g; Sodium 199 mg; Carbs 1.85 g; Fibre 0.1 g; Sugar 0.02 g; Protein 50.06 g

Thyme Roasted ChickenThyme Roasted Chicken

Prep Time: 10 minutes| **Cook Time:** 60 minutes| **Serves:** 6

1 (1.8kg) chicken
2 teaspoons dried thyme
1 teaspoon garlic powder
½ teaspoon onion powder
2 teaspoons dried parsley
1 teaspoon baking powder
1 medium lemon
2 tablespoons salted butter, melted

1. Rub chicken with thyme, garlic powder, onion powder, parsley, and baking powder. 2. Slice lemon and place four slices on top of chicken, breast side up, and secure with toothpicks. Place remaining slices inside of the chicken. 3. Place entire chicken into the air fryer basket, breast side down. 4. Adjust the temperature to 175°C and set the timer for 60 minutes. 5. After 30 minutes, flip chicken so breast side is up. 6. When done, internal temperature should be 75°C and the skin golden and crispy. To serve, pour melted butter over entire chicken.
Per Serving: Calories 363; Fat 10.74 g; Sodium 248 mg; Carbs 1.18 g; Fibre 0.2 g; Sugar 0.23 g; Protein 61.67 g

Lime Chicken Thighs

Prep Time: 15 minutes| **Cook Time:** 22 minutes| **Serves:** 4

4 bone-in, skin-on chicken thighs
1 teaspoon baking powder
½ teaspoon garlic powder
2 teaspoons chili powder
1 teaspoon cumin
2 medium limes
5g chopped fresh coriander

1. Pat the chicken thighs dry and then sprinkle them with baking powder. 2. Mix garlic powder, chili powder, and cumin in a small bowl and sprinkle the mixture evenly over the chicken thighs, gently rubbing on and under chicken skin. 3. Cut one lime in half and squeeze juice over thighs. Place chicken into the air fryer basket. 4. Adjust the temperature to 195°C and set the timer for 22 minutes. 5. Cut other lime into four wedges for serving and garnish cooked chicken with wedges and coriander.
Per Serving: Calories 441; Fat 32.4 g; Sodium 198 mg; Carbs 4.15 g; Fibre 0.7 g; Sugar 0.5 g; Protein 32.34 g

Chicken Taquitos

Prep Time: 15 minutes| **Cook Time:** 10 minutes| **Serves:** 6

Olive oil
200g fat-free cream cheese, softened
30ml Buffalo sauce
280g shredded cooked chicken
12 (18cm) low-carb flour tortillas

1. Spray an air fryer basket lightly with olive oil. 2. In a large bowl, mix together the cream cheese and Buffalo sauce until well-combined. Add the chicken and stir until combined. 3. Place the tortillas on a clean workspace. Spoon 2 to 3 tablespoons of the chicken mixture in a thin line down the centre of each tortilla. Roll up the tortillas. 4. Place the tortillas in the fryer basket, seam side down. Spray each tortilla lightly with olive oil. Cook the taquitos in batches as needed. 5. Air fry at 180°C until golden brown, for 5 to 10 minutes.
Per Serving: Calories 283; Fat 8.02 g; Sodium 371 mg; Carbs 29.66 g; Fibre 2.8 g; Sugar 4.59 g; Protein 23.14 g

Crispy Chicken TendersCrispy Chicken Tender

Prep Time: 15 minutes| **Cook Time:** 20 minutes| **Serves:** 4

445g boneless, skinless chicken mini fillets
60ml hot sauce
35g grated parmesan
1 teaspoon chili powder
1 teaspoon garlic powder

1. In a large bowl, place the boneless chicken mini fillets and pour hot sauce over them. Toss tenders in hot sauce, evenly coating. 2. Mix grated parmesan with chili powder and garlic powder in a second large bowl. 3. Place each tender in the parmesan covering completely. Press down the parmesan into the chicken with wet hands. 4. Place the tenders in a single layer into the air fryer basket. 5. Adjust the temperature to 190°C and set the timer for 20 minutes. 6. Serve warm.
Per Serving: Calories 160; Fat 5.1 g; Sodium 492 mg; Carbs 1.15 g; Fibre 0.3 g; Sugar 0.25 g; Protein 26.01 g

Simple Turkey Tenderloin

Prep Time: 20 minutes| **Cook Time:** 30 minutes| **Serves:** 4

Olive oil
½ teaspoon paprika
½ teaspoon garlic powder
½ teaspoon salt
½ teaspoon freshly ground black pepper
Pinch cayenne pepper
675g turkey breast tenderloin

1. Spray an air fryer basket lightly with olive oil. 2. In a small bowl, combine the paprika, garlic powder, salt, black pepper, and cayenne pepper. Rub the mixture all over the turkey. 3. Place the turkey in the air fryer basket and lightly spray with olive oil. 4. Air fry at 185°C for 15 minutes. Flip the turkey over and lightly spray with olive oil. Air fry until the internal temperature reaches at least 75°C for an additional 10 to 15 minutes. 5. Let the turkey rest for 10 minutes before slicing and serving.
Per Serving: Calories 264; Fat 4.79 g; Sodium 460 mg; Carbs 0.9 g; Fibre 0.3 g; Sugar 0.09 g; Protein 51.44 g

Mexican Sheet Pan Chicken Supper

Prep Time: 10 minutes| **Cook Time:** 15 minutes| **Serves:** 4

450g boneless, skinless chicken tenderloins, cut into strips
3 peppers, any colour, cut into chunks
1 onion, cut into chunks
1 tablespoon olive oil, plus more for spraying
1 tablespoon fajita seasoning mix

1. In a large bowl, mix together the chicken, peppers, onion, 1 tablespoon of olive oil, and fajita seasoning mix until completely coated. 2. Spray an air fryer basket lightly with olive oil. 3. Place the chicken and vegetables in the fryer basket and lightly spray with olive oil. 4. Air fry at 185°C for 7 minutes. Shake the basket and cook until the chicken is cooked through and the veggies are starting to char, an additional 5 to 8 minutes.
Per Serving: Calories 203; Fat 6.57 g; Sodium 249 mg; Carbs 10.69 g; Fibre 1.5 g; Sugar 6.11 g; Protein 24.49 g

Apricot-Glazed Turkey Tenderloin

Prep Time: 20 minutes| **Cook Time:** 30 minutes| **Serves:** 4

Olive oil
80g sugar-free apricot preserves
½ tablespoon spicy brown mustard
675g turkey breast tenderloin
Salt
Freshly ground black pepper

1. Spray an air fryer basket lightly with olive oil. 2. Combine the apricot preserves and mustard in a small bowl to make a paste. 3. Season the turkey with salt and pepper. Spread the apricot paste all over the turkey. 4. Place the turkey in the air fryer basket and lightly spray with olive oil. 5. Air fry at 185°C for 15 minutes. Flip the turkey over and lightly spray with olive oil. Air fry until the internal temperature reaches at least 75°C, an additional 10 to 15 minutes. 6. Let the glazed turkey rest for 10 minutes before slicing and serving.
Per Serving: Calories 263; Fat 4.75 g; Sodium 235 mg; Carbs 0.54 g; Fibre 0.2 g; Sugar 0.02 g; Protein 51.45 g

Turkey Burgers

Prep Time: 40 minutes| **Cook Time:** 20 minutes| **Serves:** 4

Olive oil
450g lean turkey mince
30g whole-wheat bread crumbs
60ml hoisin sauce
2 tablespoons soy sauce
4 whole-wheat buns

1. Spray an air fryer basket lightly with olive oil. 2. In a large bowl, mix together the turkey, bread crumbs, hoisin sauce, and soy sauce. 3. Make 4 equal patties out from the mixture. Cover with plastic wrap and refrigerate the patties for 30 minutes. 4. Place the patties in the fryer basket in a single layer. Spray the patties lightly with olive oil. 5.Air fry at 185°C for 10 minutes. Flip the patties over, lightly spray with olive oil, and cook until golden brown, an additional 5 to 10 minutes. 6. Add the patties onto buns and top with your choice of low-calorie burger toppings like sliced tomatoes, onions, and cabbage slaw.
Per Serving: Calories 340; Fat 13.65 g; Sodium 631 mg; Carbs 29.29 g; Fibre 3 g; Sugar 6.55 g; Protein 25.98 g

Savory Sesame Chicken Tenders

Prep Time: 5 minutes, plus 2 hours to marinate| **Cook Time:** 15 minutes| **Serves:** 4

Olive oil
60ml soy sauce
2 tablespoons white vinegar
1 tablespoon honey
1 tablespoon toasted sesame oil
1 tablespoon lime juice
1 teaspoon ground ginger
450g boneless skinless, chicken tenderloins
2 teaspoon toasted sesame seeds

1. Spray an air fryer basket lightly with olive oil. 2. In a large zip-top plastic bag, combine the soy sauce, white vinegar, honey, sesame oil, lime juice, and ginger to make a marinade. 3. Add the chicken tenderloins to the bag, seal, and marinate the chicken in the refrigerator for at least 2 hours or overnight. 4. Thread 1 chicken tenderloin onto each skewer. Sprinkle with sesame seeds. Reserve the marinade. (For wooden skewers, soak them in water for at least 30 minutes.) 5. Place the skewers in the fryer basket in a single layer. You may need to cook the chicken in batches. 6.Air fry at 190°C for 6 minutes. Flip the chicken over, baste with more marinade, and cook until crispy, an additional 5 to 8 minutes.
Per Serving: Calories 237; Fat 9.91 g; Sodium 307 mg; Carbs 9.34 g; Fibre 0.6 g; Sugar 7.5 g; Protein 26.61 g

Teriyaki Chicken and Broccoli Bowls

Prep Time: 5 minutes, plus up to 30 minutes to marinate| **Cook Time:** 15 minutes| **Serves:** 4

Olive oil
80ml soy sauce
110g honey
3 tablespoons white vinegar
1½ teaspoons dried thyme
1½ teaspoons paprika
1 teaspoon ground black pepper
½ teaspoon cayenne pepper
½ teaspoon ground allspice
450g boneless, skinless chicken tenderloins
300g cooked brown rice
180g steamed broccoli florets

1. Spray an air fryer basket lightly with olive oil. 2. Mix together the soy sauce, honey, white vinegar, thyme, paprika, black pepper, cayenne pepper, and allspice in a large bowl to make a marinade. 3. Add the tenderloins to the marinade and stir to coat. Cover and refrigerate for 30 minutes. 4. Place the chicken in the fryer basket in a single layer. Cook the chicken in batches as needed. Reserve the marinade. 5. Air fry at 190°C for 6 minutes. Turn the chicken over and brush with some of the remaining marinade. Cook until chicken reaches an internal temperature of at least 75°C, an additional 5 to 7 minutes. 6. To assemble the bowls, place 80 g of brown rice, 45 g of steamed broccoli, and 2 chicken tenderloins into each bowl and serve.
Per Serving: Calories 402; Fat 7.89 g; Sodium 386 mg; Carbs 53.19 g; Fibre 3.4 g; Sugar 27.61 g; Protein 29.91 g

Turkey-bread Meatballs

Prep Time: 15 minutes| **Cook Time:** 15 minutes| **Serves:** 6

Olive oil
450g lean turkey mince
55g panko bread crumbs
1 egg, beaten
1 tablespoon soy sauce
60ml plus 1 tablespoon hoisin sauce, divided
2 teaspoons minced garlic
⅛ teaspoon salt
⅛ teaspoon freshly ground black pepper
1 teaspoon sriracha

1. Spray an air fryer basket lightly with olive oil. 2. Mix together the turkey, panko bread crumbs, egg, soy sauce, 1 tablespoon of hoisin sauce, garlic, salt, and black pepper in a large bowl. 3. Using a tablespoon, form 24 meatballs. 4. Combine the remaining 60 ml of hoisin sauce and sriracha in a small bowl to make a glaze and set aside. 5. Place the meatballs in the fryer basket in a single layer. You may need to cook them in batches. 6. Air fry at 175°C for 8 minutes. Generously brush the glaze over the meatballs and cook until cooked through, an additional 4 to 7 minutes.
Per Serving: Calories 184; Fat 8.45 g; Sodium 238 mg; Carbs 10.12 g; Fibre 0.6 g; Sugar 1.05 g; Protein 16.88 g

Cheddar Stuffed Peppers

Prep Time: 20 minutes| **Cook Time:** 15 minutes| **Serves:** 4

225g lean turkey mince
4 medium peppers
1 (375g) can black beans, drained and rinsed
100g shredded reduced-fat Cheddar cheese
200g cooked long-grain brown rice
250g mild salsa
1¼ teaspoons chili powder
1 teaspoon salt
½ teaspoon ground cumin
½ teaspoon freshly ground black pepper
Olive oil
Chopped fresh coriander, for garnish

1. In a large skillet over medium-high heat, cook the turkey, breaking it up with a spoon, until browned, about 5 minutes. Drain off any excess fat. 2. Cut about 1 cm off the tops of the peppers and then cut in half lengthwise. Remove and discard the seeds and set the peppers aside. 3. In a large bowl, combine the browned turkey, black beans, Cheddar cheese, rice, salsa, chili powder, salt, cumin, and black pepper. Spoon the mixture into the peppers. 4. Lightly spray an air fryer basket with olive oil. 5. Place the stuffed peppers in the air fryer basket. Air fry at 180°C until heated throughout, 10 to 15 minutes. Garnish with coriander and serve.
Per Serving: Calories 263; Fat 9.33 g; Sodium 1399 mg; Carbs 24.29 g; Fibre 4.5 g; Sugar 5.83 g; Protein 22.82 g

Parmesan-crumb Chicken

Prep Time: 1 hour 10 minutes| **Cook Time:** 20 minutes| **Serves:** 4

1 egg
2 tablespoons lemon juice
2 teaspoons minced garlic
½ teaspoon salt
½ teaspoon freshly ground black pepper
4 boneless, skinless chicken breasts, thin cut
Olive oil
55g whole-wheat bread crumbs
25g grated Parmesan cheese

1. In a medium bowl, whisk together the egg, lemon juice, garlic, salt, and black pepper. Add the chicken breasts, cover, and refrigerate for up to 1 hour. 2. Combine the Parmesan cheese together with bread crumbs in a shallow bowl. 3. Spray an air fryer basket lightly with olive oil. 4. Remove the chicken breasts from the egg mixture, then dredge them in the bread crumb mixture, and place in the air fryer basket in a single layer. Lightly spray the chicken breasts with olive oil. You may need to cook the chicken in batches. 5. Air fry at 180°C for 8 minutes. Flip the chicken over, lightly spray with olive oil, and cook until the chicken reaches an internal temperature of 75°C, for an additional 7 to 12 minutes.
Per Serving: Calories 516; Fat 14.24 g; Sodium 789 mg; Carbs 12.2 g; Fibre 0.7 g; Sugar 1.27 g; Protein 79.56 g

Balsamic Chicken and Veggies

Prep Time: 10 minutes| **Cook Time:** 30 minutes| **Serves:** 4

180ml balsamic vinaigrette dressing, divided
450g boneless, skinless chicken tenderloins
Olive oil
450g fresh green beans, trimmed
340g grape tomatoes

1. Place 120 ml of the balsamic vinaigrette dressing and the chicken in a large zip-top plastic bag, seal, and refrigerate for at least 1 hour or up to overnight. 2. Mix together the green beans, tomatoes, and the remaining 60 ml of balsamic vinaigrette dressing in a large bowl until well coated. 3. Spray the fryer basket lightly with olive oil. Place the vegetables in the fryer basket. Reserve any remaining vinaigrette. 4. Air fry at 185°C to 205°C for 8 minutes. Shake the air fryer basket and continue to cook until the beans are crisp but tender, and the tomatoes are soft and slightly charred, an additional 5 to 7 minutes. 5. Wipe the fryer basket with a paper towel and spray lightly with olive oil. 6. Place the chicken in the fryer basket in a single layer. Cook them in batches as needed. 7. Air fry at 185°C to 205°C for 7 minutes. Flip the chicken over, baste with some of the remaining vinaigrette, and cook until the chicken reaches an internal temperature of 75°C, an additional 5 to 8 minutes. 8. Serve the chicken and veggies together.
Per Serving: Calories 188; Fat 4.62 g; Sodium 97 mg; Carbs 11.66 g; Fibre 4.6 g; Sugar 5.66 g; Protein 26.02 g

Chicken Wraps

Prep Time: 1 hour 10 minutes| **Cook Time:** 15 minutes| **Serves:** 4

450g boneless, skinless chicken tenderloins
135g jerk marinade
Olive oil
4 large low-carb tortillas
130g julienned carrots
120g peeled cucumber ribbons
35g shredded lettuce
165g mango or pineapple chunks

1. In a medium bowl, coat the chicken with the jerk marinade, cover, and refrigerate for 1 hour. 2. Spray a fryer basket lightly with olive oil. 3. Place the chicken in the fryer basket in a single layer and spray lightly with olive oil. You may need to cook the chicken in batches. Reserve any leftover marinade. 4. Air fry at 190°C for 8 minutes. Turn the chicken over and brush with some of the remaining marinade. Cook the chicken until the internal chicken part reaches at least 75°C, an additional 5 to 7 minutes. 5. To assemble the wraps, fill each tortilla with 35 g carrots, 30 g cucumber ribbons, 10 g lettuce, and 40 g mango. Place one quarter of the chicken tenderloins on top and roll up the tortilla. These are great served warm or cold.
Per Serving: Calories 425; Fat 16.73 g; Sodium 1072 mg; Carbs 38.83 g; Fibre 4.6 g; Sugar 20.02 g; Protein 30.17 g

Spinach, Cheese and Chicken Meatballs

Prep Time: 30 minutes| **Cook Time:** 18 minutes| **Serves:** 6

Olive oil
100g fresh spinach, chopped
½ teaspoon salt, plus more as needed
55g panko bread crumbs
¼ teaspoon freshly ground black pepper
¼ teaspoon garlic powder
1 egg, beaten
450g chicken mince
80g crumbled feta cheese

1. Spray a large skillet lightly with olive oil. Add the spinach, season lightly with salt, and cook over medium heat until the spinach has wilted, for 2 to 3 minutes. Set aside. 2. In a large bowl, mix together the panko bread crumbs, ½ teaspoon of salt, black pepper, and garlic powder. Add the egg, chicken, spinach, and feta cheese and stir to gently combine. 3. Using a heaping tablespoon, form 24 meatballs. 4. Lightly spray a fryer basket with olive oil. 5. Then place the meatballs in the air fryer basket in a single layer. Spray the meatballs lightly with olive oil. Cook them in batches as needed. 6. Air fry at 175°C for 7 minutes. Turn the meatballs over and cook until golden brown, an additional 5 to 8 minutes.
Per Serving: Calories 193; Fat 9.59 g; Sodium 340 mg; Carbs 9.55 g; Fibre 0.7 g; Sugar 0.48 g; Protein 17.22 g

Breaded Chicken Strips

Prep Time: 15 minutes| **Cook Time:** 20 minutes| **Serves:** 4

1 tablespoon of olive oil, plus more for spraying
450g boneless, skinless chicken tenderloins
1 teaspoon salt
½ teaspoon freshly ground black pepper
½ teaspoon paprika
½ teaspoon garlic powder
55g seasoned bread crumbs
1 teaspoon dried parsley

1. Spray an air fryer basket lightly with olive oil. 2. Toss the chicken with the salt, black pepper, paprika, and garlic powder in a medium bowl until evenly coated. 3. Add the olive oil and toss to coat the chicken evenly. 4. In a separate, shallow bowl, mix together the bread crumbs and parsley. 5. Coat each piece of chicken evenly in the bread crumb mixture. 6. Transfer the chicken tenderloins to the air fryer basket in a single layer and spray it lightly with olive oil. Cook them in batches as needed. 7. Air fry at 185°C for 10 minutes. Flip the chicken over, lightly spray with olive oil, and cook until golden brown, an additional 8 to 10 minutes.
Per Serving: Calories 216; Fat 7.31 g; Sodium 868 mg; Carbs 10.94 g; Fibre 1 g; Sugar 0.91 g; Protein 25.32 g

Dijon Roasted Turkey Breast

Prep Time: 20 minutes| **Cook Time:** 45 minutes| **Serves:** 6

1 tablespoon olive oil, plus more for spraying
2 garlic cloves, minced
2 teaspoons Dijon mustard
1½ teaspoons rosemary
1½ teaspoons sage
1½ teaspoons thyme
1 teaspoon salt
½ teaspoon freshly ground black pepper
1.3kg turkey breast, thawed if frozen

1. Spray an air fryer basket lightly with olive oil. 2. Mix together the garlic, olive oil, Dijon mustard, rosemary, sage, thyme, salt, and black pepper in a small bowl for a paste. Smear the paste all over the turkey breast. 3. Place the turkey breast in the fryer basket. 4. Air fry at 185°C for 20 minutes. Flip turkey breast over and baste it with any drippings that have collected in the bottom drawer of the air fryer. Air fry the turkey breast until the internal temperature of the meat reaches at least 75°C, 20 more minutes. 5. If desired, increase the temperature to 205°C, flip the turkey breast over one last time, and air fry for up to 5 minutes to get a crispy exterior. 6. Let the turkey rest for 10 minutes before slicing and serving.
Per Serving: Calories 380; Fat 18.28 g; Sodium 540 mg; Carbs 0.75 g; Fibre 0.3 g; Sugar 0.03 g; Protein 49.83 g

Spinach and Feta-Stuffed Chicken Breast

Prep Time: 15 minutes| **Cook Time:** 25 minutes| **Serves:** 2

1 tablespoon unsalted butter
125g frozen spinach, thawed and drained
½ teaspoon garlic powder, divided
½ teaspoon salt, divided
40g chopped yellow onion
60g crumbled feta
2 (150g) boneless, skinless chicken breasts
1 tablespoon coconut oil

1. Set a suitable frying pan over medium heat, add butter to the pan and sauté spinach for 3 minutes. Sprinkle ¼ teaspoon garlic powder and ¼ teaspoon salt onto spinach and add onion to the pan. 2. Continue sautéing 3 more minutes, then remove from heat and place in medium bowl. Fold feta into spinach mixture. 3. Slice a roughly 10 cm slit into the side of each chicken breast, lengthwise. Spoon half of the mixture into each piece and secure closed with a couple toothpicks. Sprinkle outside of chicken with remaining garlic powder and salt. Drizzle with coconut oil. Place chicken breasts into the air fryer basket. 4. Adjust the temperature to 175°C and set the timer for 25 minutes. 5. When completely cooked chicken should be golden brown and have an internal temperature of at least 75°C. Slice and serve warm.

Per Serving: Calories 327; Fat 24.1 g; Sodium 864 mg; Carbs 5.19 g; Fibre 2.3 g; Sugar 1.73 g; Protein 23.44 g

Black Pepper Chicken with Celery

Prep Time: 10 minutes| **Cook Time:** 15 minutes| **Serves:** 4

Olive oil
120ml soy sauce
2 tablespoons hoisin sauce
4 teaspoons minced garlic
1 teaspoon freshly ground black pepper
8 boneless, skinless chicken tenderloins
120g chopped celery
1 medium red pepper, diced

1. Spray an air fryer basket lightly with olive oil. 2. Mix together the hoisin sauce, garlic, soy sauce, and black pepper in a large bowl to make a marinade. Add the chicken, celery, and pepper and toss to coat. 3. Shake the excess marinade off the chicken, place it and the vegetables in the air fryer basket, and lightly spray with olive oil. Cook them in batches as needed. Reserve the remaining marinade. 4. Air fry at 190°C for 8 minutes. Turn the chicken over and brush with some of the remaining marinade. Cook until the chicken reaches an internal temperature of at least 75°C, an additional 5 to 7 minutes.

Per Serving: Calories 193; Fat 8.14 g; Sodium 658 mg; Carbs 15.29 g; Fibre 2.1 g; Sugar 9.95 g; Protein 14.23 g

Chapter 5 Beef, Pork, and Lamb Recipes

Pork Tenderloin with Mustard

Prep Time: 5 minutes| **Cook Time:** 20 minutes| **Serves:** 6

55g mayonnaise
2 tablespoons Dijon mustard
½ teaspoon dried thyme
¼ teaspoon dried rosemary
1 (450g) pork tenderloin
½ teaspoon salt
¼ teaspoon ground black pepper

1. Mix mayonnaise, mustard, thyme, and rosemary in a small bowl. 2. Brush tenderloin with mixture on all sides, then sprinkle with salt and pepper on all sides. 3. Place tenderloin into an ungreased air fryer basket. 4. Adjust the temperature setting to 205°C and set the timer for 20 minutes, turning tenderloin halfway through cooking. 5. Tenderloin will be golden and have an internal temperature of at least 60°C when done. 6. Serve warm.
Per Serving: Calories 144; Fat 6g; Sodium 372mg; Carbs 0.8g; Fibre 0.4g; Sugar 0.2g; Protein 20.6g

Wrapped Pork Tenderloin

Prep Time: 10 minutes| **Cook Time:** 20 minutes| **Serves:** 6

1 (450g) pork tenderloin
½ teaspoon salt
½ teaspoon garlic powder
¼ teaspoon ground black pepper
8 slices sugar-free bacon

1. Sprinkle tenderloin with salt, garlic powder, and pepper. 2. Wrap each piece of bacon around tenderloin and secure it with toothpicks.3. Place tenderloin into an ungreased air fryer basket. 4. Adjust the temperature setting to 205°C and set the timer for 20 minutes, turning tenderloin after 15 minutes. Bacon will be crispy and tenderloin will have an internal temperature of at least 60°C when done. 5. Cut the tenderloin into six even portions and transfer each to a medium plate. 6. Serve warm.
Per Serving: Calories 110; Fat 2.66g; Sodium 237mg; Carbs 0.37g; Fibre 0.1g; Sugar 0.1g; Protein 20g

Butter Pork Chops

Prep Time: 5 minutes| **Cook Time:** 12 minutes| **Serves:** 4

4 (100g) boneless pork chops
½ teaspoon salt
¼ teaspoon ground black pepper
2 tablespoons salted butter, softened

1. Sprinkle pork chops on all sides with salt and pepper. 2. Place chops into an ungreased air fryer basket in a single layer. 3. Adjust the temperature setting to 205°C and set the timer for 12 minutes. 4. Pork chops will be golden and have an internal temperature of at least 60°C when done. 5. Use tongs to remove cooked pork chops from your air fryer and place onto a large plate. 6. Top each chop with ½ tablespoon butter and sit for 2 minutes to melt. 7. Serve warm.
Per Serving: Calories 71; Fat 4.79g; Sodium 5185mg; Carbs 0.3g; Fibre 0g; Sugar 0g; Protein 6.5g

Marinated Steak Kebabs

Prep Time: 45 minutes| **Cook Time:** 5 minutes| **Serves:** 4

450g strip steak, fat trimmed, cut into 2.5 cm cubes
120ml soy sauce
60ml olive oil
1 tablespoon granular brown sweetener
½ teaspoon salt
¼ teaspoon ground black pepper
1 medium green pepper, chopped into 2.5 cm cubes without seeds

1. Place the steak into a large sealable bowl or bag, pour in soy sauce and olive oil, add sweetener, then stir them to coat the steak. 2. Marinate the steak at room temperature for 30 minutes (or in the refrigerator for 24 hours). 3. Remove steak from marinade and sprinkle with salt and black pepper. 4. Chop the steak into 2.5 cm cubes. 5. Place them and vegetables onto 15 cm skewer sticks, alternating between steak and pepper. 6. Place kebabs into an ungreased air fryer basket. Adjust the temperature setting to 205°C and set the timer for 5 minutes. It will be done when the meat edges are crispy and peppers are tender. 8. Serve warm.

Per Serving: Calories 457; Fat 31g; Sodium 1296mg; Carbs 9g; Fibre 0.9g; Sugar 7g; Protein 35g

Cheese-Stuffed Steak Burgers

Prep Time: 10 minutes| **Cook Time:** 10 minutes| **Serves:** 4

450g sirloin mince
100g mild Cheddar cheese, cubed
½ teaspoon salt
¼ teaspoon ground black pepper

1. Form sirloin mince into four equal balls, separate each ball in half and flatten into two thin patties (eight total patties). 2. Add 25 g Cheddar cheese into the centre of one patty and top with a second patty, press edges to seal the burger closed. 3. Repeat with remaining patties and Cheddar to create four burgers. 4. Sprinkle salt and pepper over both sides of burgers and carefully place burgers into ungreased air fryer basket. 5. Adjust the temperature setting to 175°C and set the timer for 10 minutes. 6. Burgers will be done when the edges and top are browned. 7. Serve warm.

Per Serving: Calories 218 ; Fat 11g; Sodium 669mg; Carbs 3.3g; Fibre 0g; Sugar 2.15g; Protein 26.15g

Mozzarella Corn Dogs Mozzarella

Prep Time: 10 minutes| **Cook Time:** 8 minutes| **Serves:** 4

170g shredded mozzarella cheese
25g cream cheese
50g blanched finely ground almond flour
4 beef hot dogs

1. Place mozzarella, cream cheese, and flour in a large microwave-safe bowl. 2. Microwave them on high for 45 seconds, then stir with a fork until a soft ball of dough forms. 3. Press dough out into a 30 cm × 15 cm rectangle, then use a knife to separate into four smaller rectangles. 4. Wrap each hot dog in one rectangular dough and place into ungreased air fryer basket. 5. Adjust the temperature to 205°C and set the timer for 8 minutes(turning corn dogs halfway through cooking). 6. Corn dogs will be golden brown when done. 7. Serve warm.

Per Serving: Calories 299; Fat 21g; Sodium 843mg; Carbs 16g; Fibre 2.5g; Sugar 1.5g; Protein 14.4g

Pork Chops Stuffed with Bacon and Cheese

Prep Time: 10 minutes| **Cook Time:** 12 minutes| **Serves:** 4

20g grated parmesan cheese
50g shredded sharp Cheddar cheese
4 slices cooked sugar-free bacon, crumbled
4 (100g) boneless pork chops
½ teaspoon salt
¼ teaspoon ground black pepper

1. Mix parmesan, cheddar cheese, and bacon in a small bowl. 2. Make a 8 cm slit in the side of each pork chop and stuff with ¼ parmesan mixture. 3. Sprinkle each side of pork chops with salt and pepper. 4. Place pork chops into an ungreased air fryer basket, stuffed side up. 5. Adjust the temperature to 205°C and set the timer for 12 minutes. Pork chops will be browned and have an internal temperature of at least 60°C when done. 6. Serve warm.
Per Serving: Calories 321; Fat 18g; Sodium 723mg; Carbs 1g; Fibre 0g; Sugar 0g; Protein 37g

Parmesan-Crusted Pork Chops

Prep Time: 5 minutes| **Cook Time:** 12 minutes| **Serves:** 4

1 large egg
50g grated Parmesan cheese
4 (100g) boneless pork chops
½ teaspoon salt
¼ teaspoon ground black pepper

1. Whisk egg in a medium bowl and place Parmesan in a separate medium bowl. 2. Sprinkle pork chops on both sides with salt and pepper. 3. Dip each pork chop into egg, then press both sides into Parmesan. 4. Place pork chops into an ungreased air fryer basket. 5. Adjust the temperature to 205°C and set the timer for 12 minutes, turning chops halfway through cooking. Pork chops will be golden and have an internal temperature of at least 60°C when done. Serve warm.
Per Serving: Calories 302; Fat 10.94g; Sodium 609mg; Carbs 2.16g; Fibre 0g; Sugar 0.18g; Protein 45.74g

Marinated Ribeye Steak

Prep Time: 35 minutes| **Cook Time:** 10 minutes| **Serves:** 4

450g ribeye steak
60ml soy sauce
1 tablespoon Worcestershire sauce
1 tablespoon granular brown sweetener
2 tablespoons olive oil
½ teaspoon salt
¼ teaspoon ground black pepper

1. Place ribeye in a large sealable bowl or bag and pour in soy sauce, Worcestershire sauce, sweetener, and olive oil. 2. Seal it and marinate it for 30 minutes in the refrigerator. 3. Remove ribeye from marinade, pat dry, and sprinkle on all sides with salt and pepper. 4. Place ribeye into an ungreased air fryer basket, adjust the temperature to 205°C, and set the timer for 10 minutes. Steak will be done when browned at the edges and has an internal temperature of 65°C for medium or 80°C for well-done. Serve warm.
Per Serving: Calories 333; Fat 23g; Sodium 733mg; Carbs 7.2g; Fibre 0.4g; Sugar 3.6g; Protein 24g

Spicy Pork Spare Ribs

Prep Time: 10 minutes| **Cook Time:** 30 minutes| **Serves:** 6

10g granular brown sweetener
2 teaspoons paprika
2 teaspoons chili powder
1 teaspoon garlic powder
½ teaspoon cayenne pepper
2 teaspoons salt
1 teaspoon ground black pepper
1 (1.8kg) rack pork spare ribs

1. Mix sweetener, paprika, chili powder, garlic powder, cayenne pepper, salt, and black pepper in a small bowl. 2. Rub spice mix over ribs on both sides. 3. Place ribs on ungreased aluminum foil sheet and wrap to cover. 4. Place ribs into an ungreased air fryer basket., adjust the temperature to 205°C and set the timer for 25 minutes. 5. When timer beeps, remove ribs from foil, then place back into the air fryer basket to cook for an additional 5 minutes, turning halfway through cooking. Ribs will be browned and have an internal temperature of at least 80°C when done. 6. Serve warm.
Per Serving: Calories 460; Fat 19g; Sodium 1165mg; Carbs 2g; Fibre 0.8g; Sugar 0g; Protein 66g

Mexican Shredded Beef

Prep Time: 5 minutes| **Cook Time:** 35 minutes| **Serves:** 6

1 (900g) beef chuck roast, cut into 5 cm cubes
1 teaspoon salt
½ teaspoon ground black pepper
125g added chipotle sauce

1. Sprinkle the beef cubes with salt and pepper and toss to coat in a large bowl. 2. Place beef into an ungreased air fryer basket. 3. Adjust the temperature setting to 205°C and set the timer for 30 minutes, shaking the basket halfway through cooking. Beef will be done when internal temperature is at least 70°C. 4. Place cooked beef into a large bowl and shred with two forks. 5. Pour in chipotle sauce and toss to coat. 6. Return beef to air fryer basket for an additional 5 minutes at 205°C to crisp with sauce. 7. Serve warm.
Per Serving: Calories 278; Fat 12.8g; Sodium 509mg; Carbs 0.35g; Fibre 0.1g; Sugar 0.19g; Protein 40.37g

Pork Meatballs

Prep Time: 10 minutes| **Cook Time:** 12 minutes| **Serves:** 6

450g pork mince
1 large egg, whisked
½ teaspoon garlic powder
½ teaspoon salt
½ teaspoon ground ginger
¼ teaspoon crushed red pepper flakes
1 medium spring onion, trimmed and sliced

1. Combine the pork mince, the whisked egg, garlic powder, salt, ginger, pepper flakes, and spring onion in a large bowl. 2. Spoon out 2 tablespoons mixture and roll into a ball, repeat to form eighteen meatballs total. 3. Place meatballs into an ungreased air fryer basket. 4. Adjust the temperature setting to 205°C and set the timer for 12 minutes, shaking the basket three times throughout cooking. Meatballs will be browned and have an internal temperature of at least 60°C when done. 5. Serve warm.
Per Serving: Calories 164; Fat 10g; Sodium 252mg; Carbs 1g; Fibre 0g; Sugar 0g; Protein 15g

London Steak

Prep Time: 2 hours | **Cook Time:** 12 minutes | **Serves:** 4

450g top round steak
1 tablespoon Worcestershire sauce
60ml soy sauce
2 cloves garlic, peeled and finely minced
½ teaspoon ground black pepper
½ teaspoon salt
2 tablespoons salted butter, melted

1. Place steak in a large sealable bowl or bag, pour in Worcestershire sauce and soy sauce, then add garlic, pepper, and salt, and toss to coat. 2. Seal it and place it into a refrigerator to marinate for 2 hours. 3. Remove steak from marinade and pat dry. 4. Drizzle top side with butter, then place into ungreased air fryer basket. 5. Adjust the temperature to 190°C and set the timer for 12 minutes, turning steak halfway through cooking. 6. Steak will be done when browned at the edges and it has an internal temperature of 65°C for medium or 80°C for well-done. 7. Rest the steak on a large plate for 10 minutes before slicing into thin pieces. 8. Serve warm.
Per Serving: Calories 271; Fat 11g; Sodium 691mg; Carbs 6g; Fibre 0g; Sugar 4g; Protein 35g

Italian Beef Meatballs

Prep Time: 10 minutes | **Cook Time:** 20 minutes | **Serves:** 4

450g beef mince
1 large egg, whisked
25g grated Parmesan cheese
½ teaspoon salt
½ teaspoon dried parsley
¼ teaspoon ground black pepper
¼ teaspoon dried oregano

1. Combine beef mince, the whisked egg, Parmesan cheese, salt, parsley, black pepper, and oregano in a large bowl. 2. Scoop out 3 tablespoons mixture and roll into a ball. 3. Repeat with remaining mixture to form sixteen balls total. 4. Place meatballs into an ungreased air fryer basket in a single layer, working in batches if needed. 5. Adjust the temperature to 205°C and set the timer for 20 minutes, shaking the basket halfway through cooking. 6. Meatballs will be browned and have an internal temperature of at least 80°C when done. 7. Serve warm.
Per Serving: Calories 284; Fat 15g; Sodium 475mg; Carbs 1g; Fibre 0g; Sugar 0g; Protein 33g

Roast Beef

Prep Time: 5 minutes | **Cook Time:** 60 minutes | **Serves:** 6

1 (900g) top round beef roast
1 teaspoon salt
½ teaspoon ground black pepper
1 teaspoon dried rosemary
½ teaspoon garlic powder
1 tablespoon coconut oil, melted

1. Sprinkle all sides of roast with salt, pepper, rosemary, and garlic powder. 2. Drizzle with coconut oil. 3. Place roast into an ungreased air fryer basket, fatty side down. 4. Adjust the temperature setting to 190°C and set the timer for 60 minutes, turning the roast halfway through cooking. Roast will be done when no pink remains and internal temperature is at least 80°C. 5. Serve warm.
Per Serving: Calories 217; Fat 9g; Sodium 479mg; Carbs 0.6g; Fibre 0.1g; Sugar 0.2g; Protein 34g

Beef and Chorizo Burger

Prep Time: 10 minutes| **Cook Time:** 15 minutes| **Serves:** 4

335g lean beef mince
110g Mexican-style ground chorizo
40g chopped onion
5 slices pickled jalapeños, chopped
2 teaspoons chili powder
1 teaspoon minced garlic
¼ teaspoon cumin

1. Mix the beef mince, ground chorizo, chopped onion, jalapenos, chili powder, garlic, and cumin in a large bowl. 2. Divide the mixture into four sections and form them into burger patties. 3. Place burger patties into the air fryer basket, working in batches if necessary. 4. Adjust the temperature setting to 190°C and set the timer for 15 minutes. 5. Flip the patties halfway through the cooking time. 6. Serve warm.
Per Serving: Calories 271; Fat 16.29g; Sodium 704mg; Carbs 4.6g; Fibre 1g; Sugar 1.68g; Protein 25.6g

Spice-Rubbed Pork Loin

Prep Time: 5 minutes| **Cook Time:** 20 minutes| **Serves:** 6

1 teaspoon paprika
½ teaspoon ground cumin
½ teaspoon chili powder
½ teaspoon garlic powder
2 tablespoons coconut oil
1 (675g) boneless pork loin
½ teaspoon salt
¼ teaspoon ground black pepper

1. Mix paprika, cumin, chili powder, and garlic powder in a small bowl. 2. Drizzle coconut oil over pork. 3. Sprinkle pork loin with salt and pepper, then rub spice mixture evenly on all sides. 4. Place pork loin into an ungreased air fryer basket. 5. Adjust the temperature to 205°C and set the timer for 20 minutes, turning pork halfway through cooking. Pork loin will be browned and have an internal temperature of at least 60°C when done. 6. Serve warm.
Per Serving: Calories 193; Fat 9g; Sodium 257mg; Carbs 1g; Fibre 0g; Sugar 0g; Protein 26g

Tender Blackened Steak Nuggets

Prep Time: 10 minutes| **Cook Time:** 7 minutes| **Serves:** 2

450g ribeye steak, cut into 2.5 cm cubes
2 tablespoons salted butter, melted
½ teaspoon paprika
½ teaspoon salt
¼ teaspoon garlic powder
¼ teaspoon onion powder
¼ teaspoon ground black pepper
⅛ teaspoon cayenne pepper

1. Place the steak into a large bowl and pour in butter, then toss to coat. 2. Sprinkle with the remaining ingredients. 3. Place steak into an ungreased air fryer basket. 4. Adjust the temperature to 205°C and set the timer for 7 minutes, shaking the basket three times during cooking. Steak will be crispy on the outside and browned when done and internal temperature is at least 65°C for medium and 80°C for well-done. 5. Serve warm.
Per Serving: Calories 498; Fat 34g; Sodium 844mg; Carbs 5.4g; Fibre 0.4g; Sugar 0.4g; Protein 44.5g

Cheese and Spinach Steak Rolls

Prep Time: 10 minutes| **Cook Time:** 12 minutes| **Serves:** 4

1 (445g) flank steak, butterflied
8 (25g, ½ cm-thick) slices provolone cheese
30g fresh spinach leaves
½ teaspoon salt
¼ teaspoon ground black pepper

1. Place steak on a large plate, then place provolone slices to cover it, leaving 2.5 cm at the edges. 2. Lay spinach leaves over cheese. 3. Gently roll steak and tie with kitchen twine or secure with toothpicks. 4. Carefully slice the steak into eight pieces. 5. Sprinkle each with salt and pepper. 6. Place rolls into ungreased air fryer basket, cut side up. 7. Adjust the temperature to 205°C and set the timer for 12 minutes. Steak rolls will be browned and cheese will be melted when done and have an internal temperature of at least 65°C for medium steak and 80°C for well-done steak. 8. Serve warm.
Per Serving: Calories 633; Fat 23g; Sodium 1428mg; Carbs 2g; Fibre 0g; Sugar 0g; Protein 98g

Bacon and Cheese Burger Casserole

Prep Time: 15 minutes| **Cook Time:** 20 minutes| **Serves:** 4

450g lean beef mince
¼ medium white onion, peeled and chopped
1 large egg
4 slices bacon, cooked and crumbled
2 pickle spears, chopped
100g shredded Cheddar cheese, divided

1. Set a frying pan over medium heat, add the beef mince and then brown for about 7–10 minutes. When no pink remains, drain the fat. 2. Remove from heat and add beef mince to a large mixing bowl. 3. Add onion, 50 g Cheddar and egg to the bowl. 4. Mix them well and add crumbled bacon. 5. Pour the mixture into a 15 cm x 5 cm round baking dish and top with remaining Cheddar. 6. Place all of them into the air fryer basket, adjust the temperature setting to 190°C and then set the time setting to 20 minutes. The casserole will be golden on top and firm in the middle when fully cooked. 7. Serve immediately with chopped pickles on top.
Per Serving: Calories 303; Fat 17g; Sodium 390mg; Carbs 0.7g; Fibre 0.2g; Sugar 0.2g; Protein 33.8g

Juicy Baked Pork Chops

Prep Time: 5 minutes| **Cook Time:** 15 minutes| **Serves:** 2

1 teaspoon chili powder
½ teaspoon garlic powder
½ teaspoon cumin
¼ teaspoon ground black pepper
¼ teaspoon dried oregano
2 (100g) boneless pork chops
2 tablespoons unsalted butter, divided

1. Mix chili powder, garlic powder, cumin, pepper and oregano in a small bowl. 2. Rub the dry rub onto pork chops. 3. Place pork chops into the air fryer basket, adjust the temperature to 205°C and set the timer for 15 minutes. The internal temperature shall reach at least 60°C when fully cooked. 4. Serve warm, each topped with 1 tablespoon butter.
Per Serving: Calories 316; Fat 14.38g; Sodium 136mg; Carbs 2.13g; Fibre 0.7g; Sugar 0.42g; Protein 42.46g

Crusted Buttery Beef Tenderloin

Prep Time: 10 minutes| **Cook Time:** 25 minutes| **Serves:** 6

2 tablespoons salted butter, melted
2 teaspoons minced roasted garlic
3 tablespoons ground 4-peppercorn blend
1 (900g) beef tenderloin, trimmed of visible fat

1. Mix the butter and roasted garlic in a small bowl. Brush it over the beef tenderloin. 2. Place the ground peppercorns onto a plate and roll the tenderloin through them, creating a crust. 3. Place tenderloin into the air fryer basket, adjust the temperature to 205°C and set the timer for 25 minutes. 4. Turn the tenderloin halfway through cooking. 5. Allow tenderloin to rest for 10 minutes before slicing.

Per Serving: Calories 343; Fat 16g; Sodium 107mg; Carbs 0.3g; Fibre 0g; Sugar 0g; Protein 46.2g

Southern-style Breaded Pork Chops

Prep Time: 10 minutes| **Cook Time:** 15 minutes| **Serves:** 4

35g grated parmesan
1 teaspoon chili powder
½ teaspoon garlic powder
1 tablespoon coconut oil, melted
4 (100g) pork chops

1. Mix parmesan, chili powder, and garlic powder in a large bowl. 2. Brush coconut oil over each pork chop and then press them into the pork rind mixture, coating both sides. 3. Place each coated pork chop into the air fryer basket, adjust the temperature setting to 205°C and then set the cooking time to 15 minutes. 4. Flip each pork chop halfway through cooking. When the pork chops are fully cooked, they should be golden on the outside and reach an internal temperature of at least 60°C. 5. Serve and enjoy!

Per Serving: Calories 120; Fat 8.5g; Sodium 41mg; Carbs 2.4g; Fibre 0.3g; Sugar 0g; Protein 10g

Lasagna Casserole

Prep Time: 15 minutes| **Cook Time:** 15 minutes| **Serves:** 4

170g no-sugar-added pasta sauce
450g lean beef mince, cooked and drained
125g full-fat ricotta cheese
25g grated Parmesan cheese
½ teaspoon garlic powder
1 teaspoon dried parsley
½ teaspoon dried oregano
110g shredded mozzarella cheese

1. Pour 55 g pasta sauce on the bottom of 15 cm x 5 cm round baking dish. 2. Place ¼ of the beef mince on top of the sauce. 3. Mix ricotta, Parmesan, garlic powder, parsley, and oregano in a small bowl. 4. Place dollops of half the mixture on top of the beef. 5. Sprinkle with ⅓ of the mozzarella. 6. Repeat layers until all beef, ricotta mixture, sauce, and mozzarella are used, ending with the mozzarella on top. 7. Cover dish with foil and place into the air fryer basket, adjust the temperature setting to 185°C and then set the timer for 15 minutes. In the last 2 minutes of cooking, remove the foil to brown the cheese. 8. Serve immediately.

Per Serving: Calories 365; Fat 16.5g; Sodium 394mg; Carbs 6g; Fibre 1.6g; Sugar 1.2g; Protein 44.6g

Air Fried Worcestershire Pork Belly

Prep Time: 40 minutes| **Cook Time:** 20 minutes| **Serves:** 4

450g pork belly, cut into 2.5 cm cubes
60ml soy sauce
1 tablespoon Worcestershire sauce
2 teaspoons sriracha hot chili sauce
½ teaspoon salt
¼ teaspoon ground black pepper

1. Place pork belly into a medium sealable bowl or bag and pour in soy sauce, Worcestershire sauce, and sriracha. 2. Seal it and let it marinate for 30 minutes in the refrigerator. 3. Remove pork from marinade, pat dry with a paper towel, and sprinkle with salt and pepper. 4. Place pork in ungreased air fryer basket, adjust the temperature to 180°C and set the timer for 20 minutes, shaking the basket halfway through cooking. 5. Pork belly will be done when it has an internal temperature of at least 60°C and is golden brown. 6. Rest pork belly on a large plate 10 minutes. 7. Serve warm.
Per Serving: Calories 188; Fat 9g; Sodium 1851mg; Carbs 6.77g; Fibre 0.4g; Sugar 5.3g; Protein 20.5g

Classic Pulled Pork

Prep Time: 10 minutes| **Cook Time:** 2½ hours| **Serves:** 8

2 tablespoons chili powder
1 teaspoon garlic powder
½ teaspoon onion powder
½ teaspoon ground black pepper
½ teaspoon cumin
1 (1.8kg) pork shoulder

1. Mix chili powder, garlic powder, onion powder, pepper, and cumin in a small bowl. 2. Rub the spice mixture over the pork shoulder, patting it into the skin. 3. Place the pork shoulder into the air fryer basket, adjust the temperature to 175°C and set the timer for 150 minutes. The pork skin will be crispy and meat easily shredded with two forks when done. The internal temperature should be at least 60°C. 4. Serve warm.
Per Serving: Calories 615; Fat 40.5g; Sodium 190mg; Carbs 1.7g; Fibre 0.8g; Sugar 0.3g; Protein 57g

Air Fryer Baby Back Ribs

Prep Time: 5 minutes| **Cook Time:** 25 minutes| **Serves:** 4

900g baby back ribs
2 teaspoons chili powder
1 teaspoon paprika
½ teaspoon onion powder
½ teaspoon garlic powder
¼ teaspoon ground cayenne pepper
120ml sugar-free barbecue sauce

1. Rub ribs with chili powder, paprika, onion powder, and cayenne pepper together. 2. Place into the air fryer basket, adjust the temperature to 205°C and set the timer for 25 minutes. Ribs will be dark and charred with an internal temperature of at least 85°C when done. 3. Brush ribs with barbecue sauce and serve warm.
Per Serving: Calories 511; Fat 36g; Sodium 186mg; Carbs 2.4g; Fibre 0.8g; Sugar 0.3g; Protein 45g

Savory Latin American-style Pastries

Prep Time: 15 minutes| **Cook Time:** 10 minutes| **Serves:** 4

450g lean beef mince
120ml water
30g diced onion
2 teaspoons chili powder
½ teaspoon garlic powder
¼ teaspoon cumin
170g shredded mozzarella cheese
50g blanched finely ground almond flour
50g full-fat cream cheese
1 large egg

1. Brown the ground beef for about 7–10 minutes in a medium frying pan over medium heat. 2. Drain the fat. Return the frying pan to the stove. Add water and onion to the frying pan. Stir and sprinkle with chili powder, garlic powder, and cumin. 3. Reduce heat and simmer for an additional 3–5 minutes. Remove from heat and set aside. 4. Add mozzarella, almond flour, and cream cheese in a large microwave-safe bowl. Microwave for 1 minute. Stir until smooth. Form the mixture into a ball. 5. Then place it between two sheets of parchment and roll out to ½ cm thickness. 6. Cut the dough into four squares. Place ¼ of beef mince onto the bottom half of each square. Fold the dough over and roll the edges up or press with a wet fork to close. 7. Crack the large egg into a small bowl and whisk. Brush the whisked egg over the pastries. 8. Cut a suitable piece of parchment to fit your air fryer basket and place the pastries on the parchment. 9. Place into the air fryer basket, adjust the temperature to 205°C and set the timer for 10 minutes. 10. Flip the pastries halfway through the cooking time. 11. Serve warm.
Per Serving: Calories 460; Fat 25.6g; Sodium 480mg; Carbs 7.9g; Fibre 2.3g; Sugar 2.7g; Protein 49.6g

Fajita Flank Steak Rolls

Prep Time: 20 minutes| **Cook Time:** 15 minutes| **Serves:** 6

2 tablespoons unsalted butter
40g diced yellow onion
1 medium red pepper
1 medium green pepper
2 teaspoons chili powder
1 teaspoon cumin
½ teaspoon garlic powder
900g flank steak
4 (25g) slices pepper jack cheese

1. Remove seeds from the peppers and slice them into strips. Melt butter and sauté onion, red pepper and green pepper in a medium frying pan over medium heat. 2. Sprinkle with chili powder, cumin, and garlic powder. Sauté until peppers are tender, for about 5–7 minutes. 3. Lay flank steak flat on a work surface. Spread onion and pepper mixture over entire steak rectangle. Lay slices of cheese on top of onions and peppers, barely overlapping. 4. With the shortest end toward you, begin rolling the steak, tucking the cheese down into the roll as necessary. 5. Secure the roll with twelve toothpicks, six on each side of the steak roll. 6. Place steak roll into the air fryer basket, adjust the temperature to 205°C and set the timer for 15 minutes. Rotate the roll halfway through cooking. 7. Add an additional 1–4 minutes depending on your preferred internal temperature (55°C for medium). 8. When the timer beeps, allow the roll to rest for 15 minutes, then slice into six even pieces. 9. Serve warm.
Per Serving: Calories 267; Fat 12.24g; Sodium 139mg; Carbs 3.02g; Fibre 1g; Sugar 1.48g; Protein 34.32g

Tender Pork Spare Ribs

Prep Time: 10 minutes| **Cook Time:** 30 minutes| **Serves:** 4

1 (1.8kg) rack pork spare ribs
1 teaspoon ground cumin
1 teaspoon ground black pepper
1 teaspoon garlic powder
½ teaspoon dry ground mustard
2 teaspoons salt
125g low-carb barbecue sauce

1. Place ribs on the ungreased aluminum foil sheet, and carefully use a knife to remove membrane. 2. Sprinkle meat evenly on both sides with cumin, salt, pepper, garlic powder, and ground mustard. 3. Cut the rack pork spare ribs into portions to fit in your air fryer, and wrap each portion in a layer of aluminum foil, working in batches if needed. 4. Place ribs into an ungreased air fryer basket, adjust the temperature to 205°C and set the timer for 25 minutes. 5. Carefully remove ribs from foil when the timer beeps and brush with barbecue sauce. 6. Return them to your air fryer and cook at 205°C for an additional 5 minutes to brown. The cooking is done when no pink remains on the ribs and the internal temperature is at least 80°C. Serve warm.
Per Serving: Calories 192; Fat 12g; Sodium 1344mg; Carbs 3g; Fibre 0g; Sugar 0g; Protein 13g

Tasty Seared Ribeye

Prep Time: 5 minutes| **Cook Time:** 45 minutes| **Serves:** 2

1 (200g) ribeye steak
½ teaspoon pink Himalayan salt
¼ teaspoon ground peppercorn
1 tablespoon coconut oil
1 tablespoon salted butter, softened
¼ teaspoon garlic powder
½ teaspoon dried parsley
¼ teaspoon dried oregano

1. Rub the salt and ground peppercorn over the steak. 2. Place into the air fryer basket, adjust the temperature to 120°C and set the timer for 45 minutes. (Or place it into the air fryer at 205°C for 10–15 minutes for quick cook. Flip halfway through.) 3. After timer beeps, check doneness and add a few minutes until internal temperature is your personal preference. 4. Add coconut oil in a medium frying pan over medium heat. When oil is hot, quickly sear outside and sides of steak until crisp and browned. 5. Remove from heat and allow steak to rest. 6. Whip butter with garlic powder, parsley, and oregano in a small bowl. 7. Slice steak and serve with herbs and butter on top.
Per Serving: Calories 327; Fat 24.8g; Sodium 722mg; Carbs 2.6g; Fibre 0.1g; Sugar 0g; Protein 24.4g

Stuffed Peppers

Prep Time: 15 minutes| **Cook Time:** 15 minutes| **Serves:** 4

450g lean beef mince
1 tablespoon chili powder
2 teaspoons cumin
1 teaspoon garlic powder
1 teaspoon salt
¼ teaspoon ground black pepper
250g drained diced tomatoes with green chili
4 medium green peppers
100g shredded Monterey jack cheese, divided

1. Brown the beef mince about 7-10 minutes in a medium frying pan over medium heat. 2. When no pink remains, drain the fat from the frying pan. 3. Return the frying pan to the stovetop and add chili powder, cumin, garlic powder, salt, and black pepper. 4. Add the drained diced tomatoes and chiles to the frying pan. 5. Continue cooking for 3-5 minutes. 6. While it is cooking, cut each pepper in half. Remove the seeds and white membrane. 7. Spoon the cooked mixture evenly into each pepper and top with a 25 g cheese. 8. Place the stuffed peppers into your air fryer basket. 9. Adjust the temperature to 175°C and set the timer for 15 minutes. Peppers will be fork tender and cheese will be browned and bubbling when done. 10. Serve warm.

Per Serving: Calories 410; Fat 23g; Sodium 919mg; Carbs 9.64g; Fibre 2g; Sugar 5g; Protein 40.5g

Crispy Stir-fried Beef and Broccoli

Prep Time: 60 minutes| **Cook Time:** 20 minutes| **Serves:** 2

225g sirloin steak, thinly sliced
2 tablespoons soy sauce (or liquid aminos)
¼ teaspoon grated ginger
¼ teaspoon finely minced garlic
1 tablespoon coconut oil
180g broccoli florets
¼ teaspoon crushed red pepper
⅛ teaspoon xanthan gum
½ teaspoon sesame seeds

1. Add soy sauce, ginger, garlic, and coconut oil into a large bowl or storage bag to marinate beef. 2. Allow to marinate for 1 hour in refrigerator. 3. Remove beef from marinade, reserving marinade 4. Place the beef into the air fryer basket, adjust the temperature to 160°C and set the timer for 20 minutes. 5. After 10 minutes, add broccoli and sprinkle red pepper into the air fryer basket and shake. 6. Transfer the marinade to a frying pan over medium heat to boil, then reduce to simmer. 7. Stir in xanthan gum and allow it to thicken. 8. When the air fryer timer beeps, quickly empty air fryer basket into the frying pan and toss. 9. Sprinkle with sesame seeds. Serve immediately.

Per Serving: Calories 333; Fat 22.4g; Sodium 315mg; Carbs 5.4g; Fibre 1.5g; Sugar 3.3g; Protein 26g

Mozzarella-Stuffed Meatloaf

Prep Time: 10 minutes| **Cook Time:** 30 minutes| **Serves:** 6

450g lean beef
½ medium green pepper, seeded and chopped
¼ medium yellow onion, peeled and chopped
½ teaspoon salt
¼ teaspoon ground black pepper
50g mozzarella cheese, sliced into ½ cm thick slices
60g ketchup

1. Combine beef mince, pepper, onion, salt, and black pepper in a large bowl. 2. Cut a suitable piece of parchment to fit your air fryer basket and place the half beef mixture on ungreased parchment (form a 23 cm × 10 cm loaf, about 1 cm thick). 3. Centre mozzarella slices on the beef loaf (leaving at least ½ cm around each edge). 4. Press the remaining beef into a second 23 cm × 10 cm loaf and place it on top of the mozzarella slices, and press the edges of the two loaves together to seal. 5. Place the meatloaf with parchment into the air fryer basket. Adjust the temperature setting to 175°C and set the timer for 30 minutes. 6. Carefully turn over the loaf and brush the top with ketchup halfway through cooking. 7. Loaf will be browned and have an internal temperature of at least 80°C when done. 8. Slice and serve warm.
Per Serving: Calories 178; Fat 8.4g; Sodium 318mg; Carbs 1g; Fibre 0.3g; Sugar 0.6g; Protein 23g

Simple Mini Meatloaf

Prep Time: 10 minutes| **Cook Time:** 25 minutes| **Serves:** 6

445g lean beef mince
¼ medium yellow onion, peeled and diced
½ medium green pepper, seeded and diced
1 large egg
3 tablespoons blanched finely ground almond flour
1 tablespoon Worcestershire sauce
½ teaspoon garlic powder
1 teaspoon dried parsley
2 tablespoons tomato paste
60ml water
1 tablespoon powdered sweetener

1. Combine beef mince, onion, pepper, egg and almond flour in a large bowl. 2. Pour in the Worcestershire sauce and add the garlic powder and parsley to the bowl, mix until fully combined. 3. Divide the mixture into two and place into two (10 cm) loaf baking pans. 4. Mix the tomato paste, water, and sweetener in a small bowl, spoon half the mixture over each loaf, working in batches if necessary, place loaf pans into the air fryer basket. 5. Adjust the temperature setting to 175°C and set the timer for 25 minutes or the until internal temperature is 80°C. 6. Serve warm.
Per Serving: Calories 205; Fat 11.56g; Sodium 80mg; Carbs 2.72g; Fibre 0.7g; Sugar 1.17g; Protein 21.83g

Chapter 6 Snack and Starter Recipes

Fried Edamame

Prep Time: 5 minutes| **Cook Time:** 10 minutes| **Serves:** 4

Olive oil
1 (400g) bag frozen edamame in pods
½ teaspoon salt
½ teaspoon garlic salt
¼ teaspoon freshly ground black pepper
½ teaspoon red pepper flakes (optional)

1.Spray an air fryer basket lightly with olive oil. 2. Add the frozen edamame in a medium bowl, lightly spray with olive oil, and toss to coat. 3. Mix together the salt, garlic salt, black pepper, and red pepper flakes (if using) in a small bowl. 4. Add the mixture to the edamame and toss until evenly coated. 5. Place half the edamame in the fryer basket, and make sure it won't be overfilled the basket. 6. Air fry at 190°C for 5 minutes. 7. Shake the basket and cook until the edamame is starting to brown and get crispy, 3 to 5 more minutes. 8. Repeat with the remaining edamame and serve immediately.
Per Serving: Calories 97; Fat 4.04g; Sodium 296mg; Carbs 33.42g; Fibre 4.1g; Sugar 1.98g; Protein 8.57g

Spicy Fried Chickpeas

Prep Time: 5 minutes| **Cook Time:** 20 minutes| **Serves:** 4

Olive oil
½ teaspoon ground cumin
½ teaspoon chili powder
¼ teaspoon cayenne pepper
¼ teaspoon salt
1 (475g) can chickpeas, drained and rinsed

1. Spray a fryer basket lightly with olive oil. 2. Combine the cumin, chili powder, cayenne pepper, and salt in a small bowl. 3. Add the chickpeas in a medium bowl and lightly spray them with olive oil. 4. Add the spice mixture and toss until coated evenly. 5. Transfer the chickpeas to the fryer basket. 6. Air fry at 200°C until the chickpeas reach your desired level of crunchiness, for 15 to 20 minutes, making sure to shake the basket every 5 minutes.
Per Serving: Calories 90; Fat 1.7g; Sodium 290mg; Carbs 14.89g; Fibre 4.2g; Sugar 2.58g; Protein 4.58g

Fried Cinnamon and Sugar Peaches

Prep Time: 10 minutes| **Cook Time:** 13 minutes| **Serves:** 4

Olive oil
2 tablespoons sugar
¼ teaspoon ground cinnamon
4 peaches, cut into wedges

1. Spray an air fryer basket lightly with olive oil. 2. In a medium bowl combine together the sugar and cinnamon, and then add the peaches and toss to coat evenly. 3. Place the peaches in a single layer in the fryer basket on their sides, and cook them in batches. 4. Air fry at 175°C for 5 minutes. 5. Turn the peaches skin side down, lightly spray them with oil, and air fry until the peaches are lightly brown and caramelized, for 5 to 8 more minutes.
Per Serving: Calories 74; Fat 0g; Sodium 0mg; Carbs 18g; Fibre 2g; Sugar 16.5g; Protein 1.4g

Bacon-Wrapped Onion Rings

Prep Time: 5 minutes| **Cook Time:** 10 minutes| **Serves:** 4

1 large onion, peeled
1 tablespoon sriracha
8 slices bacon

1. Slice onion into ½ cm thick slices. 2. Brush sriracha over the onion slices. 3. Take two slices of onion and wrap bacon around the rings. 4. Repeat with remaining onion and bacon. 5. Place it into the air fryer basket. 6. Adjust the temperature to 175°C and set the timer for 10 minutes. 7. Use tongs to flip the onion rings halfway through the cooking time. 8. Serve it warm.
Per Serving: Calories 105; Fat 0.04g; Sodium 2mg; Carbs 3.5g; Fibre 0.6g; Sugar 2g; Protein 7g

Mini Sweet Pepper Bacon Poppers

Prep Time: 15 minutes| **Cook Time:** 8 minutes| **Serves:** 4

8 mini sweet peppers
200g full-fat cream cheese, softened
4 slices bacon, cooked and crumbled
30g shredded pepper jack cheese

1. Remove the tops from the peppers and slice each one in half lengthwise. 2. Use a small knife to remove seeds and membranes. 3. Mix cream cheese, bacon, and pepper jack in a small bowl. 4. Place 3 teaspoons of the mixture into each sweet pepper and press it down smooth. Place into the air fryer basket. 5. Adjust the temperature to 205°C and set the timer for 8 minutes. 6. Serve it warm.
Per Serving: Calories 233; Fat 11.12g; Sodium 336mg; Carbs 25.98g; Fibre 3.3g; Sugar 1.69g; Protein 10.86g

Fluffy Cheese Bread

Prep Time: 10 minutes| **Cook Time:** 10 minutes| **Serves:** 2

110g shredded mozzarella cheese
25g grated Parmesan cheese
1 large egg
½ teaspoon garlic powder

1. Mix all ingredients in a large bowl. 2. Cut a piece of parchment to fit your air fryer basket. 3. Press the mixture into a circle on the parchment and put it into the air fryer basket. 4. Adjust the temperature to 175°C and set the timer for 10 minutes. 5. Serve it warm.
Per Serving: Calories 162; Fat 5.74g; Sodium 650mg; Carbs 4.6g; Fibre 1.1g; Sugar 0.91g; Protein 22.94g

Simple Five Spice Crunchy Edamame

Prep Time: 5 minutes| **Cook Time:** 16 minutes| **Serves:** 4

95g ready-to-eat edamame, shelled
1 tablespoon sesame oil
1 teaspoon five spice powder
½ teaspoon salt

1. Preheat air fryer at 175°C for 3 minutes. 2.Toss edamame in sesame oil in a small bowl. 3. Place it in your air fryer basket cooking for 5 minutes. 4. Shake. Cook an additional 5 minutes. 5. Shake again. Cook an additional 6 minutes. 6. Transfer it to a small bowl and toss it with five spice powder and salt. 7. Let it cool for serving.
Per Serving: Calories 46; Fat 3.42g; Sodium 291mg; Carbs 3.62g; Fibre 0.2g; Sugar 0.04g; Protein 0.28g

Fried Black Bean Corn Dip

Prep Time: 10 minutes| **Cook Time:** 10 minutes| **Serves:** 4

½ (375g) can black beans, drained and rinsed
½ (375g) can corn, drained and rinsed
70g chunky salsa
50g reduced-fat cream cheese, softened
25g shredded reduced-fat Cheddar cheese
½ teaspoon ground cumin
½ teaspoon paprika
Salt
Freshly ground black pepper

1. Mix together the black beans, corn, salsa, cream cheese, Cheddar cheese, cumin, and paprika in a medium bowl. 2. Add salt and the freshly ground black pepper to season the mixture and stir until well combined. 3. Spoon the mixture into an air fryer–safe baking dish. 4. Place baking dish in the fryer basket and air fry at 160°C until heated through, for about 10 minutes. 5. Serve hot.

Per Serving: Calories 105; Fat 4.98g; Sodium 427mg; Carbs 12.86g; Fibre 1.4g; Sugar 3.52g; Protein 4.16g

Crunchy Tortilla Chips

Prep Time: 5 minutes| **Cook Time:** 5 minutes| **Serves:** 4

Olive oil
½ teaspoon salt
½ teaspoon ground cumin
½ teaspoon chili powder
½ teaspoon paprika
Pinch cayenne pepper
8 (15cm) corn tortillas, each cut into 6 wedges

1. Spray fryer basket lightly with olive oil. 2. Combine the salt, cumin, chili powder, paprika, and cayenne pepper in a small bowl. 3. Place the tortilla wedges in the fryer basket in a single layer. 4. Spray the tortillas lightly with oil and sprinkle with some of the seasoning mixture. 5. Cook the tortillas in batches. 6. Air fry at 190°C for 2 to 3 minutes. 7. Shake the basket and cook until the chips are light brown and crispy, an additional 2 to 3 minutes. Watch the chips closely to avoid burning.

Per Serving: Calories 3; Fat 0.15g; Sodium 301mg; Carbs 0.46g; Fibre 0.3g; Sugar 0.06g; Protein 0.14g

Courgette Chips

Prep Time: 10 minutes| **Cook Time:** 15 minutes| **Serves:** 4

Olive oil
2 large courgettes, cut into ¼ cm-thick slices
2 teaspoons Cajun seasoning

1. Spray a fryer basket lightly with olive oil. 2. Put the courgette slices in a medium bowl and spray them generously with olive oil. 3. Sprinkle the Cajun seasoning over the courgette and stir to make sure they are evenly coated with oil and seasoning. 4. Place slices in a single layer in the fryer basket, making sure not to overcrowd but cook these in several batches. 5. Air fry at 185°C for 8 minutes. 6. Flip the slices over and air fry until they are as crisp and brown as you prefer, for an additional 7 to 8 minutes.

Per Serving: Calories 6; Fat 0.03g; Sodium 103mg; Carbs 1.08g; Fibre 0.3g; Sugar 0.15g; Protein 0.28g

Thinly Sliced Beef Jerky

Prep Time: 5 minutes| **Cook Time:** 4 hours| **Serves:** 10

450g flat iron beef, thinly sliced
60ml soy sauce (or liquid aminos)
2 teaspoons Worcestershire sauce
¼ teaspoon crushed red pepper flakes
¼ teaspoon garlic powder
¼ teaspoon onion powder

1. Place all ingredients into a plastic storage bag or covered container and marinate them for 2 hours in refrigerator. 2. Place each slice of jerky on the air fryer rack in a single layer. 3. Adjust the temperature to 70°C and set the timer for 4 hours. 4. Cool and store it in airtight container up to 1 week.
Per Serving: Calories 80; Fat 3.47g; Sodium 145mg; Carbs 2.02g; Fibre 0.2g; Sugar 1.41g; Protein 10.24g

Italian Mozzarella Sticklets

Prep Time: 15 minutes| **Cook Time:** 10 minutes| **Serves:** 6

2 tablespoons all-purpose flour
1 large egg
1 tablespoon whole milk
55g plain bread crumbs
¼ teaspoon salt
¼ teaspoon Italian seasoning
10 mozzarella sticks, each cut into thirds
2 teaspoons olive oil

1. Add flour in a small bowl. Whisk egg and milk together in another small bowl. 2. Combine bread crumbs, salt, and Italian seasoning in a shallow dish. 3. Roll a mozzarella sticklet in flour, dredge it in egg mixture, and then roll in bread crumb mixture. 4. Shake off excess between each step. 5. Set it aside on a plate and repeat with remaining mozzarella. Place it in freezer for 10 minutes. 6. To prepare, heat your air fryer at 205°C for about 3 minutes. 7. Place half of mozzarella sticklets in fryer basket cooking for 2 minutes. 8. Shake it and lightly brush it with olive oil cooking for an additional 2 minutes. Shake again cooking for an additional 1 minute. 9. Transfer it to a serving dish. Repeat with remaining sticklets and serve warm.
Per Serving: Calories 68; Fat 2.75g; Sodium 173mg; Carbs 8.63g; Fibre 0.5g; Sugar 0.59g; Protein 1.92g

Simple Bone Marrow Butter

Prep Time: 10 minutes| **Cook Time:** 12 minutes| **Serves:** 4

900g beef bone marrow bones, cut into 5 cm sections
2 cloves garlic, peeled and quartered
5 tablespoons butter, softened
1 tablespoon chopped fresh thyme leaves
¼ teaspoon salt

1. Soak bones in water in a large bowl and refrigerate for 1 hour. 2. Preheat air fryer at 205°C for 3 minutes. 3. Place bones in ungreased air fryer basket, and cook for 12 minutes. 4. Remove it from basket and let it cool for 10 minutes. 5. Push marrow out of bones with a small knife or chopstick. 6. Add a food processor with remaining ingredients and pulse it until smooth. 6. Place mixture on a piece of plastic wrap. 7. Fold sides in to create a log. 8. Spin ends until log is tight. 9. Refrigerate for 1 hour until firm.
Per Serving: Calories 611; Fat 37.93g; Sodium 412mg; Carbs 0.65g; Fibre 0.1g; Sugar 0.03g; Protein 63.47g

Spicy Air-Fryer Sunflower Seeds

Prep Time: 10 minutes| **Cook Time:** 10 minutes| **Serves:** 4

280g unsalted sunflower seeds
2 teaspoons olive oil
2 teaspoons chili garlic paste
¼ teaspoon salt
1 teaspoon granular sweetener

1. Preheat air fryer at 160°C for 3 minutes. 2. Combine all ingredients in a medium bowl until seeds are well coated. 3. Place seeds in ungreased air fryer basket cooking for 5 minutes, and shake basket cooking for an additional 5 minutes. 4. Transfer it to a medium serving bowl and serve it.
Per Serving: Calories 815; Fat 73.15g; Sodium 169mg; Carbs 30.37g; Fibre 7.3g; Sugar 13.51g; Protein 22.53g

Air-Fryer Jalapeño Poppers

Prep Time: 10 minutes| **Cook Time:** 18 minutes| **Serves:** 6

1 tablespoon olive oil
115g pork mince
2 tablespoons pitted and finely diced Kalamata olives
2 tablespoons feta cheese
25g cream cheese, room temperature
½ teaspoon dried mint leaves
6 large jalapeños, sliced in half lengthwise and seeded

1. Heat olive oil over medium-high heat 30 seconds in a medium frying pan. 2. Add pork and cook it for 6 minutes until it is no longer pink. Drain fat. 3. Preheat air fryer to 175°C for 3 minutes. 4. Combine cooked pork, olives, feta cheese, cream cheese, and mint leaves in a medium bowl. 5. Press pork mixture into peppers. 6. Place half of poppers in ungreased air fryer basket for 6 minutes. 7. Transfer it to a medium serving plate and repeat cooking with remaining poppers. 8. Serve it warm.
Per Serving: Calories 108; Fat 8.91g; Sodium 138mg; Carbs 0.78g; Fibre 0.1g; Sugar 0.54g; Protein 6.05g

Roasted Jack-O'-Lantern Seeds with black pepper

Prep Time: 10 minutes| **Cook Time:** 13 minutes| **Serves:** 4

235g fresh pumpkin seeds
1 tablespoon butter, melted
1 teaspoon salt, divided
½ teaspoon onion powder
½ teaspoon dried parsley
½ teaspoon garlic powder
½ teaspoon dried dill
¼ teaspoon dried chives
¼ teaspoon dry mustard
¼ teaspoon celery seed
¼ teaspoon freshly ground black pepper

1. Preheat air fryer at 160°C for 3 minutes. 2. Toss seeds with butter and ½ teaspoon salt in a medium bowl. 3. Place seed mixture in ungreased air fryer basket cooking for 7 minutes. 4. Use a spatula turning seeds, and then cook for an additional 6 minutes. 5. Transfer it to a medium serving bowl, and toss it with remaining ingredients. 6. Serve it.
Per Serving: Calories 368; Fat 31.91g; Sodium 760mg; Carbs 9.44g; Fibre 4g; Sugar 0.8g; Protein 17.82g

Simple Baked Brie with Orange Marmalade and Spiced Walnuts

Prep Time: 10 minutes| **Cook Time:** 22 minutes| **Serves:** 6

120g walnuts
1 large egg white, beaten
⅛ teaspoon ground cumin
⅛ teaspoon cayenne pepper
1 teaspoon ground cinnamon
¼ teaspoon powdered sweetener
1 (200g) round Brie
2 tablespoons sugar-free orange marmalade

1. Preheat air fryer at 160°C for 3 minutes. 2. Combine walnuts with egg white in a small bowl, and set aside. 3. Combine cumin, cayenne pepper, cinnamon, and sweetener in a separate small bowl, adding walnuts, drained of excess egg white, and toss them. 4. Place walnuts in ungreased air fryer basket cooking for 6 minutes, and then toss nuts cooking for an additional 6 minutes. 5. Transfer them to a small bowl and cool it about 5 minutes until it's easy to handle. After it's cooled, chop it into smaller bits. 6. Adjust air fryer temperature to 205°C, and put Brie in an ungreased pizza pan or on a piece of parchment paper cut to size of air fryer basket cook for 10 minutes. 7. Transfer Brie to a medium serving plate and garnish it with orange marmalade and spiced walnuts.
Per Serving: Calories 661; Fat 55.97g; Sodium 1083mg; Carbs 3.03g; Fibre 1.1g; Sugar 1.17g; Protein 38.07g

Air-Fryer Avocado Fries

Prep Time: 10 minutes| **Cook Time:** 10 minutes| **Serves:** 2

1 large egg, beaten
25g almond flour
2 tablespoons ground flaxseed
¼ teaspoon chipotle powder
¼ teaspoon salt
1 large avocado, peeled, pitted, and sliced into 8 "fries"

1. Preheat air fryer to 190°C for 3 minutes. 2. Place egg in a small dish, and combine almond flour, flaxseed, chipotle powder, and salt in a separate shallow dish. 3. Dip avocado slices into egg. 4. Dredge through flour mixture to coat. 5. Place half of slices in air fryer basket lightly greased with olive oil cooking for 5 minutes. 6. Transfer it to a medium serving plate and repeat cooking with remaining avocado slices. 7. Serve it warm.
Per Serving: Calories 244; Fat 21.41g; Sodium 305mg; Carbs 11.89g; Fibre 9.6g; Sugar 0.88g; Protein 5.27g

Tasty Ranch Roasted Almonds

Prep Time: 5 minutes| **Cook Time:** 6 minutes| **Serves:** 8

315g raw almonds
2 tablespoons unsalted butter, melted
½ (25g) ranch dressing mix packet

1. Toss almonds in butter to evenly coat in a large bowl. 2. Sprinkle ranch mix over almonds and toss them. 3. Place almonds into the air fryer basket. 4. Adjust the temperature to 160°C and set the timer for 6 minutes. 5. Shake the basket two or three times during cooking. 6. Cool it at least 20 minutes. 7. Store it in an airtight container up to 3 days.
Per Serving: Calories 19; Fat 2.08g; Sodium 1mg; Carbs 0.06g; Fibre 0g; Sugar 0.01g; Protein 0.18g

Crispy Chicken Wings

Prep Time: 10 minutes| **Cook Time:** 15 minutes| **Serves:** 4

Olive oil
2 tablespoons Old Bay seasoning
2 teaspoons baking powder
2 teaspoons salt
900g chicken wings, pat dry with paper towel

1. Spray an air fryer basket lightly with olive oil. 2. Mix together the Old Bay seasoning, baking powder, and salt in a large zip-top plastic bag. 3. Place the wings in the zip-top bag, seal, and toss with the seasoning mixture until evenly coated. 4. Place the seasoned wings in the air fryer basket in a single layer. 5. Lightly spray with olive oil, and cook them in batches. 6. Air fry at 205°C for 7 minutes. 7. Turn the wings over, lightly spray them with olive oil, and air fry until the wings are crispy and lightly browned, for 5 to 8 more minutes. 8. Using a meat thermometer, check to make sure the internal temperature is 75°C or higher.
Per Serving: Calories 289; Fat 8.1g; Sodium 1347mg; Carbs 0.67g; Fibre 0.2g; Sugar 0g; Protein 49.9g

Prosciutto-Wrapped Asparagus

Prep Time: 10 minutes| **Cook Time:** 10 minutes| **Serves:** 4

450g asparagus
12 (15g) slices prosciutto
1 tablespoon coconut oil, melted
2 teaspoons lemon juice
⅛ teaspoon red pepper flakes
35g grated Parmesan cheese
2 tablespoons salted butter, melted

1. Place an asparagus spear onto a slice of prosciutto on a clean work surface. 2. Drizzle with coconut oil and lemon juice. 3. Sprinkle it with red pepper flakes and Parmesan across asparagus. 4. Roll prosciutto around asparagus spear. 5. Place them into the air fryer basket. 6. Adjust the temperature to 190°C and set the timer for 10 minutes. 7. Drizzle the asparagus roll with butter before serving.
Per Serving: Calories 201; Fat 14.3g; Sodium 481mg; Carbs 7.7g; Fibre 2.4g; Sugar 3.2g; Protein 12.4g

Fried Bacon-Wrapped Jalapeño Poppers

Prep Time: 15 minutes| **Cook Time:** 12 minutes| **Serves:** 4

6 jalapeños (about 10 cm long each)
75g full-fat cream cheese
35g shredded medium Cheddar cheese
¼ teaspoon garlic powder
12 slices bacon

1. Cut the tops off of the jalapeños and slice down the centre lengthwise into two pieces. 2. Use a knife to carefully remove white membrane and seeds from peppers. 3. Place cream cheese, Cheddar, and garlic powder in a large microwave-safe bowl. 4. Microwave for 30 seconds and stir it. 5. Spoon cheese mixture into hollow jalapeños. 6. Wrap a slice of bacon around each jalapeño half, completely covering pepper. 7. Place it into the air fryer basket. 8. Adjust the temperature to 205°C and set the timer for 12 minutes. 9. Turn the peppers halfway through the cooking time. 10. Serve it warm.
Per Serving: Calories 405; Fat 37g; Sodium 504mg; Carbs 4g; Fibre 0g; Sugar 2.8g; Protein 14g

Fried Parmesan Chicken Wings

Prep Time: 5 minutes| **Cook Time:** 25 minutes| **Serves:** 4

900g raw chicken wings
1 teaspoon pink Himalayan salt
½ teaspoon garlic powder
1 tablespoon baking powder
4 tablespoons unsalted butter, melted
35g grated Parmesan cheese
¼ teaspoon dried parsley

1. Place chicken wings, salt, ½ teaspoon garlic powder, and baking powder in a large bowl, and then toss it. 2. Place wings into the air fryer basket. 3. Adjust the temperature to 205°C and set the timer for 25 minutes. 4. Then toss the basket several times during the cooking time. 5. Combine butter, Parmesan, and parsley in a small bowl. 6. Remove wings from the air fryer and place them into a clean large bowl. 7. Pour the butter mixture over the wings and toss it until coated. 6. Serve it warm.
Per Serving: Calories 393; Fat 18.05g; Sodium 338mg; Carbs 1.69g; Fibre 0.1g; Sugar 0.02g; Protein 57.3g

Spicy Fried Buffalo Chicken Dip

Prep Time: 10 minutes| **Cook Time:** 10 minutes| **Serves:** 4

140g cooked, diced chicken breast
200g full-fat cream cheese, softened
120g buffalo sauce
80ml full-fat ranch dressing
85g chopped pickled jalapeños
150g shredded medium Cheddar cheese, divided
2 spring onions, sliced on the bias

1. Place chicken into a large bowl. 2. Add the dressing, sauce, and cheese in it. 3. Stir them until the sauces are well mixed and mostly smooth. 4. Fold in jalapeños and 100 g Cheddar. 5. Pour the mixture into a 15 cm x 5cm baking dish and place remaining Cheddar on top. 6. Place dish into the air fryer basket. 7. Adjust the temperature to 175°C and set the timer for 10 minutes. 8. When done, the top will be brown and the dip bubbling. 9. Top it with sliced spring onions. 10. Serve it warm.
Per Serving: Calories 276; Fat 16.12g; Sodium 939mg; Carbs 28.61g; Fibre 0.4g; Sugar 19.24g; Protein 4.97g

Bacon Jalapeño Cheese Bread

Prep Time: 10 minutes| **Cook Time:** 15 minutes| **Serves:** 4

225g shredded mozzarella cheese
25g grated Parmesan cheese
65g chopped pickled jalapeños
2 large eggs
4 slices bacon, cooked and chopped

1. Mix all ingredients in a large bowl. 2. Cut a piece of parchment to fit your air fryer basket. 3. Dampen your hands with a bit of water and press out the mixture into a circle. 4. Separate this into two smaller cheese breads, depending on the size of your air fryer. 5. Place the parchment and cheese bread into the air fryer basket. 5. Adjust the temperature to 160°C and set the timer for 15 minutes. 6. Carefully flip the bread when 5 minutes remain. 7. When fully cooked, the top will be golden brown. 8. Serve it warm.
Per Serving: Calories 237; Fat 12.71g; Sodium 868mg; Carbs 6.69g; Fibre 1.1g; Sugar 3.21g; Protein 24.07g

Fried Cinnamon Apple Chips

Prep Time: 10 minutes| **Cook Time:** 10 minutes| **Serves:** 4

Olive oil
2 apples, any variety, cored, cut in half, and cut into thin slices
2 heaped teaspoons ground cinnamon

1. Spray an air fryer basket lightly with oil. 2. Toss the apple slices with the cinnamon until evenly coated in a medium bowl. 3. Place the apple slices in the fryer basket in a single layer, and cook them in batches. 4. Air fry at 175°C for 4 to 5 minutes. 5. Shake the basket and cook until crispy, for another 4 to 5 minutes.
Per Serving: Calories 3; Fat 0.02g; Sodium 0mg; Carbs 1.05g; Fibre 0.7g; Sugar 0.03g; Protein 0.05g

Mozzarella-Stuffed Buffalo Meatballs

Prep Time: 15 minutes| **Cook Time:** 15 minutes| **Serves:** 4

450g lean beef mince
25g blanched finely ground almond flour
1 teaspoon dried parsley
½ teaspoon garlic powder
¼ teaspoon onion powder
1 large egg
75g low-moisture, whole-milk mozzarella, cubed
110g no-sugar-added pasta sauce
25g grated Parmesan cheese

1. Add beef mince, almond flour, parsley, garlic powder, onion powder, and egg in a large bowl. 2. Fold ingredients together until fully combined. 3. Form the mixture into 5 cm balls and use your thumb or a spoon to create an indent in the centre of each meatball. 4. Place a cube of cheese in the centre and form the ball around it. 5. Place the meatballs into the air fryer, working in batches if necessary. 6. Adjust the temperature to 175°C and set the timer for 15 minutes. (Meatballs will be slightly crispy on the outside and fully cooked when at least 80°C internally.) 7. Toss the meatballs in the sauce and sprinkle them with grated Parmesan for serving.
Per Serving: Calories 360; Fat 20.25g; Sodium 190mg; Carbs 8.98g; Fibre 1g; Sugar 5g; Protein 34.89g

Mozzarella Cheese Sticks

Prep Time: 60 minutes| **Cook Time:** 10 minutes| **Serves:** 4

6 (25g) mozzarella string cheese sticks
50g grated Parmesan cheese
1 teaspoon dried parsley
2 large eggs

1. Place mozzarella sticks on a cutting board and cut it in half. 2. Freeze it for 45 minutes until it's firm, or remove frozen sticks after 1 hour if freezing overnight, and place into airtight zip-top storage bag and put back in freezer for future use. 3. Mix Parmesan and parsley in a large bowl. 4. Whisk eggs in a medium bowl. 5. Dip a frozen mozzarella stick into beaten eggs and then into Parmesan mixture to coat. 6. Repeat with remaining sticks. 7. Place mozzarella sticks into the air fryer basket. 8. Adjust the temperature setting to 205°C and set the timer for 10 minutes or until it's golden. 9. Serve it warm.
Per Serving: Calories 87; Fat 5.99g; Sodium 233mg; Carbs 2.06g; Fibre 0g; Sugar 0.06g; Protein 5.99g

Spinach Artichoke Dip

Prep Time: 10 minutes| **Cook Time:** 10 minutes| **Serves:** 6

250g frozen spinach, drained and thawed
1 (350g) can artichoke hearts, drained and chopped
65g chopped pickled jalapeños
200g full-fat cream cheese, softened
55g full-fat mayonnaise
55g full-fat sour cream
½ teaspoon garlic powder
25g grated Parmesan cheese
105g shredded pepper jack cheese

1. Mix all ingredients in baking bowl. Place it into the air fryer basket. 2. Adjust the temperature to 160°C and set the timer for 10 minutes. 3. Remove it when brown and bubbling. 4. Serve it warm.
Per Serving: Calories 255; Fat 17.49g; Sodium 498mg; Carbs 13.82g; Fibre 3.9g; Sugar 4.6g; Protein 12.81g

Simple Mozzarella Pizza Crust

Prep Time: 5 minutes| **Cook Time:** 10 minutes| **Serves:** 1

55g shredded whole-milk mozzarella cheese
2 tablespoons blanched finely ground almond flour
1 tablespoon full-fat cream cheese
1 large egg white

1. Place cream cheese, mozzarella, and almond flour, and cream cheese in a medium microwave-safe bowl. Microwave it for 30 seconds. 2. Stir them until smooth ball of dough forms. 3. Add egg white and stir them until soft round dough forms. 4. Press into a 6 round pizza crust. Cut a piece of parchment to fit your air fryer basket and place crust on the parchment. 5. Put it into the air fryer basket. Adjust the temperature setting to 175°C and set the timer for 10 minutes. 6. Flip it after 5 minutes and place any desired toppings on the crust. 7. Continue cooking until it's golden. 8. Serve it immediately.
Per Serving: Calories 323; Fat 24.42g; Sodium 463mg; Carbs 6.08g; Fibre 1.8g; Sugar 2.53g; Protein 21.08g

Three-Meat Pizza

Prep Time: 5 minutes| **Cook Time:** 5 minutes| **Serves:** 1

55g shredded mozzarella cheese
7 slices pepperoni
35g cooked sausage meat
2 slices bacon, cooked and crumbled
1 tablespoon grated Parmesan cheese
2 tablespoons, sugar-free pizza sauce, for dipping

1. Cover the bottom of a 15 cm x 5 cm cake pan with mozzarella. 2. Place pepperoni, sausage, and bacon on top of cheese and sprinkle it with Parmesan. 3. Place pan into the air fryer basket. 4. Adjust the temperature to 205°C and set the timer for 5 minutes. 5. Remove it when cheese is bubbling and golden. 6. Serve it warm with pizza sauce for dipping.
Per Serving: Calories 335; Fat 16.66g; Sodium 1135mg; Carbs 12.21g; Fibre 1.1g; Sugar 8.07g; Protein 34.29g

Bacon-Wrapped Brie

Prep Time: 5 minutes| **Cook Time:** 10 minutes| **Serves:** 8

4 slices bacon
1 (200g) round Brie

1. Place two slices of bacon to form an X. 2. Put the third slice of bacon horizontally across the centre of the X. 2. Put the fourth slice of bacon vertically across the X, and make sure it looks like a plus sign (+) on top of an X. 3. Place the Brie in the centre of the bacon. 4. Wrap the bacon around the Brie, securing with a few toothpicks. 5. Cut a piece of parchment to fit your air fryer basket and place the bacon-wrapped Brie on top. 6. Put it inside the air fryer basket. Adjust the temperature setting to 205°C and set the timer for 10 minutes. 7. Flip Brie carefully when 3 minutes remain. 8. Finally, bacon will be crispy and cheese will be soft and melty. 9. Cut it into eight slices for serving.
Per Serving: Calories 428; Fat 35.43g; Sodium 805mg; Carbs 0.58g; Fibre 0g; Sugar 0.58g; Protein 0.58g

Smoky Roasted Almonds

Prep Time: 5 minutes| **Cook Time:** 6 minutes| **Serves:** 4

160g raw almonds
2 teaspoons coconut oil
1 teaspoon chili powder
¼ teaspoon cumin
¼ teaspoon smoked paprika
¼ teaspoon onion powder

1. Toss all ingredients in a large bowl until almonds are evenly coated with oil and spices. 2. Place almonds into the air fryer basket. 3. Adjust the temperature to 160°C and set the timer for 6 minutes. 4. Toss the air fryer basket halfway through the cooking time, and allow it to cool completely.
Per Serving: Calories 230; Fat 20g; Sodium 20mg; Carbs 8g; Fibre 4.8g; Sugar 1.6g; Protein 7.7g

Italian Pepperoni Pizza Bread

Prep Time: 5 minutes| **Cook Time:** 20 minutes| **Serves:** 4

2 large eggs, beaten
2 tablespoons coconut flour
2 tablespoons cassava flour
80g whipping cream
35g chopped pepperoni
35g grated mozzarella cheese
2 teaspoons Italian seasoning
½ teaspoon baking powder
⅛ teaspoon salt
2 tablespoons grated Parmesan cheese
110g no-sugar-added marinara sauce, warmed

1. Preheat air fryer at 150°C for 3 minutes. 2. Combine eggs with coconut flour, cassava flour, whipping cream, pepperoni, mozzarella cheese, Italian seasoning, baking powder, and salt in a medium bowl. 3. Pour batter into an ungreased pizza pan. 4. Place the pan in an air fryer basket cooking for 19 minutes. 5. Sprinkle Parmesan cheese on top for an additional minute. 6. Remove pan from basket and let it set for 5 minutes, then slice it and serve it with warmed marinara sauce.
Per Serving: Calories 81; Fat 4.09g; Sodium 308mg; Carbs 5.45g; Fibre 0.6g; Sugar 1.04g; Protein 5.38g

Italian Salsa Verde

Prep Time: 10 minutes| **Cook Time:** 10 minutes| **Serves:** 6

340g fresh tomatillos, husked
1 large jalapeño, stem removed
1 bunch (approximately 8) spring onions, both ends trimmed
3 cloves garlic, peeled
½ teaspoon salt
1 tablespoon fresh lime juice
5g fresh coriander leaves

1. Preheat air fryer at 205°C for 3 minutes. 2. Place tomatillos and jalapeño in ungreased air fryer basket, and cook for 5 minutes. 3. Add spring onions and garlic to basket, and cook for an additional 5 minutes. 4. Add tomatillos, jalapeño, spring onions, and garlic to a food processor or blender. 5. Add salt, lime juice, and coriander leaves, and pulse or blend until ingredients are finely chopped. 6. Pour it into a small sealable container and refrigerate until ready to use, up to five days.
Per Serving: Calories 22; Fat 0.6g; Sodium 195mg; Carbs 4.23g; Fibre 1.2g; Sugar 2.35g; Protein 0.71g

Jalapeño Popper

Prep Time: 10 minutes| **Cook Time:** 18 minutes| **Serves:** 4

80g riced cauliflower
2 medium jalapeños, seeded and minced
1 large egg
30g grated sharp Cheddar cheese
25g cream cheese, room temperature
1 tablespoon peeled and grated yellow onion
30g almond flour
½ teaspoon salt
¼ teaspoon garlic powder

1. Preheat air fryer at 190°C for 3 minutes. 2. Combine all ingredients in a medium bowl. Form it into twelve rectangular mounds (about 1 tablespoon each). 3. Cut a piece of parchment paper to fit bottom of air fryer basket. 4. Place six pieces on parchment paper in basket, and cook for 9 minutes. 5. Transfer it to a medium serving plate and repeat cooking with remaining pieces. 6. Let it rest for 5 minutes, and then serve it warm.
Per Serving: Calories 42; Fat 3.27g; Sodium 330mg; Carbs 1.8g; Fibre 0.5g; Sugar 0.77g; Protein 1.65g

Tasty Cauliflower Pizza Crusts

Prep Time: 10 minutes| **Cook Time:** 24 minutes| **Serves:** 2

110g cauliflower rice
1 large egg
55g grated mozzarella cheese
1 tablespoon grated Parmesan cheese
1 clove garlic, peeled and minced
1 teaspoon Italian seasoning
⅛ teaspoon salt

1. Preheat air fryer at 205°C for 3 minutes. 2. Combine cauliflower rice, the large egg, mozzarella cheese, Parmesan cheese, garlic, Italian seasoning, and salt in a medium bowl. 3. Divide mixture in half and spread it into two pizza pans greased with cooking spray. 4. Place one pizza pan in air fryer basket and cook it for 12 minutes. 5. Remove pan from basket and repeat cooking with second pan.
Per Serving: Calories 98; Fat 3.11g; Sodium 535mg; Carbs 5.64g; Fibre 1.8g; Sugar 1.66g; Protein 12.2g

Almond and Mozzarella Cheese Pizza Rolls

Prep Time: 15 minutes| **Cook Time:** 10 minutes| **Serves:** 8

225g shredded mozzarella cheese
50g almond flour
2 large eggs
72 slices pepperoni
8 (25g) mozzarella string cheese sticks, cut into 3 pieces each
2 tablespoons unsalted butter, melted
¼ teaspoon garlic powder
½ teaspoon dried parsley
2 tablespoons grated Parmesan cheese

1. Place mozzarella and almond flour in a large microwave-safe bowl. Microwave it for 1 minute. 2. Remove bowl and mix it until ball of dough forms. Microwave it additional 30 seconds if necessary. 3. Crack eggs into the bowl and mix them until smooth dough ball forms. 4. Get your hands wet with water and knead the dough briefly. Use nonstick cooking spray to spray one side of each with nonstick cooking spray. 5. Place the dough ball between the two sheets of parchment paper, with sprayed sides facing dough. 6. Roll dough out to ½ cm thickness. Use a knife to slice into 24 rectangles. 7. Place 3 pepperoni slices and 1 piece string cheese on each rectangle. 8. Fold the rectangle in half, covering pepperoni and cheese filling. Pinch or roll sides closed. 9. Cut a piece of parchment to fit your air fryer basket and place it into the basket. 10. Put the rolls onto the parchment. Adjust the temperature setting to 175°C and set the timer for 10 minutes. 11. Open the air fryer and flip the pizza rolls after 5 minutes. Restart the air fryer and continue cooking until pizza rolls are golden. 12. Place butter, garlic powder, and parsley in a small bowl. Brush the mixture over cooked pizza rolls and then sprinkle it with Parmesan. 13. Serve warm.
Per Serving: Calories 166; Fat 11.27g; Sodium 553mg; Carbs 1.41g; Fibre 0.5g; Sugar 0.45g; Protein 14.26g

Air-Fryer Barbecue Turnip Chips

Prep Time: 10 minutes| **Cook Time:** 24 minutes| **Serves:** 2

½ teaspoon smoked paprika
¼ teaspoon chili powder
¼ teaspoon garlic powder
⅛ teaspoon onion powder
⅛ teaspoon cayenne pepper
⅛ teaspoon granular sweetener
1 teaspoon salt, divided
1 large turnip, sliced into ¼ cm-thick circles
2 teaspoons olive oil

1. Preheat air fryer to 205°C for 3 minutes. 2. Combine paprika, chili powder, garlic powder, onion powder, cayenne pepper, sweetener, and ½ teaspoon salt in a small bowl, and set aside. 3. Toss turnip slices with olive oil and ½ teaspoon salt in a medium bowl. 4. Place half of turnip slices in air fryer basket lightly greased with olive oil and cook for 6 minutes. 5. Shake basket and cook for an additional 6 minutes. 6. Transfer chips to a medium bowl and repeat cooking with remaining turnip slices. 7. Toss with seasoning mix. 8. Let rest 15 minutes, then serve it.
Per Serving: Calories 46; Fat 4.71g; Sodium 1179mg; Carbs 0.98g; Fibre 0.4g; Sugar 0.12g; Protein 0.31g

Delicious Deviled Eggs

Prep Time: 5 minutes| **Cook Time:** 15 minutes| **Serves:** 4

4 large eggs
215g ice cubes
240ml water
2 tablespoons plain Greek yogurt
2 tablespoons pitted and finely chopped Kalamata olives
2 tablespoons goat cheese crumbles
⅛ teaspoon salt
⅛ teaspoon freshly ground black pepper
2 tablespoons finely chopped fresh mint

1. Preheat air fryer at 120°C for 3 minutes. 2. Place eggs in silicone muffin cups to avoid bumping around and cracking during cooking process. 3. Add silicone cups to air fryer basket cooking for 15 minutes. 4. Add ice and water to a medium bowl. 5. Transfer eggs to water bath immediately to stop cooking process. 6. After 5 minutes, carefully peel eggs. Cut eggs in half lengthwise. Spoon yolks into a separate medium bowl. Arrange white halves on a large plate. Using a fork, blend egg yolks with yogurt, olives, goat cheese, salt, and pepper. 7. Spoon mixture into white halves. 8. Garnish it with mint and serve it.
Per Serving: Calories 300; Fat 18.08g; Sodium 180mg; Carbs 8.57g; Fibre 1.7g; Sugar 2.55g; Protein 8.57g

California Deviled Eggs

Prep Time: 5 minutes| **Cook Time:** 15 minutes| **Serves:** 4

4 large eggs
215g ice cubes
240ml water
2 tablespoons mayonnaise
½ teaspoon coconut aminos
¼ medium ripe avocado, peeled, pitted, and diced
¼ teaspoon wasabi powder
2 tablespoons diced cucumber
60g lump crabmeat, shells discarded
1 sheet nori, sliced
8 slices jarred pickled ginger
1 teaspoon toasted sesame seeds

1. Preheat air fryer at 120°C for 3 minutes. 2. Place eggs in silicone muffin cups to avoid bumping around and cracking during cooking process. 3. Add silicone cups to air fryer basket cooking for 15 minutes. 4. Add ice and water to a medium bowl. Transfer eggs to water bath immediately to stop cooking process. After 5 minutes, peel eggs carefully. Cut eggs in half lengthwise. 5. Spoon yolks into a medium bowl. Arrange white halves on a large plate. 6. Using a fork, blend egg yolks, mayonnaise, coconut aminos, avocado, and wasabi powder until smooth. Mix in diced cucumber. 7. Spoon into white halves. 8. Garnish eggs with crabmeat, nori, and pickled ginger. 9. Sprinkle it with sesame seeds and serve it.
Per Serving: Calories 204; Fat 13.63g; Sodium 95mg; Carbs 16.2g; Fibre 3.5g; Sugar 4.96g; Protein 5.67g

Mexican Fried Potato Skins

Prep Time: 10 minutes| **Cook Time:** 55 minutes| **Serves:** 6

Olive oil
6 medium russet potatoes, scrubbed
Salt
Freshly ground black pepper
230g fat-free refried black beans
1 tablespoon taco seasoning
145g salsa
75g reduced-fat shredded Cheddar cheese

1. Lightly spray an air fryer basket with olive oil. 2. Spritz the potatoes lightly with oil and season with salt and pepper. 3. Pierce each potato a few times with a fork. 4. Place the potatoes in the air fryer basket, and air fry at 205°C until fork tender, for 30 to 40 minutes. 5. Meanwhile, mix together the beans and taco seasoning in a small bowl. 6. Set them aside until the potatoes are cool enough to handle. 7. Cut each potato in half lengthwise. 8. Then scoop out most of the insides, leaving about ½ cm in the skins so the potato skins hold their shape. 9. Season the insides of the potato skins with salt and black pepper. 10. Lightly spritz the insides of the potato skins with oil, and cook them in batches. 11. Place them into the air fryer basket, skin side down, and air fry until crisp and golden, for 8 to 10 minutes. 12. Transfer the potato skins to a work surface and spoon ½ tablespoon of seasoned refried black beans into each one. 13. Top each with 2 teaspoons salsa and 1 tablespoon shredded Cheddar cheese. 14. Place filled potato skins in the air fryer basket in a single layer, and lightly spray with oil. 15. Air fry them until the cheese is melted and bubbly, for 2 to 3 minutes.
Per Serving: Calories 361; Fat 1.66g; Sodium 587mg; Carbs 74.48g; Fibre 7.2g; Sugar 3.62g; Protein 14.37g

Bacon Cheeseburger Dip

Prep Time: 20 minutes| **Cook Time:** 10 minutes| **Serves:** 6

200g full-fat cream cheese
55g full-fat mayonnaise
55g full-fat sour cream
40g chopped onion
1 teaspoon garlic powder
1 tablespoon Worcestershire sauce
125g shredded medium Cheddar cheese, divided
225g cooked lean beef mince
6 slices bacon, cooked and crumbled
2 large pickle spears, chopped

1. Add cream cheese in a large microwave-safe bowl and microwave it for 45 seconds. 2. Stir it with mayonnaise, sour cream, onion, garlic powder, Worcestershire sauce, and 100 g Cheddar. 3. Add cooked beef mince and bacon. 4. Sprinkle remaining Cheddar on top. 5. Place it in 6 bowls and put them into the air fryer basket. 6. Adjust the temperature setting to 205°C and set the timer for 10 minutes. 7. Dip it when top is golden and bubbling. 8. Sprinkle pickles over dish. 9. Serve it warm.
Per Serving: Calories 231; Fat 14.24g; Sodium 473mg; Carbs 7.57g; Fibre 0.6g; Sugar 3.12g; Protein 17.63g

Chapter 7 Dessert Recipes

Perfect Beignets

Prep Time: 15 minutes | **Cook Time:** 6 minutes | **Serves:** 9

Oil, for greasing and spraying
375g plain flour, plus more for dusting
1½ teaspoons salt
1 (2¼-teaspoon) envelope active dry yeast
240ml milk
2 tablespoons packed light brown sugar
1 tablespoon unsalted butter
1 large egg
120g icing sugar

1. Sprinkle some oil in a big bowl. 2. Mix together the flour, salt, and yeast in a small bowl. 3. Pour the milk into a glass measuring cup and microwave in 1-minute intervals until it boils. 4. Mix together the brown sugar and butter. Pour in the hot milk in a bowl and whisk until the sugar has dissolved. Let cool to room temperature. 5. Whisk the egg into the cooled milk mixture and fold in the flour mixture until a dough forms. 6. On a lightly floured work surface, knead the dough for 3 to 5 minutes. 7. Place the dough in the oiled bowl and cover with a clean kitchen towel. Let rise in a warm place for about 1 hour. 8. Roll the dough out on a lightly floured work surface until it's about ½ cm thick. Cut the dough into 7.5 cm squares and place them on a lightly floured baking sheet. Cover loosely with a kitchen towel and let rise for about 30 minutes until doubled in size. 9. Line the air fryer basket with parchment and sprinkle with oil. 10. Place the dough squares in the air fryer basket and sprinkle with oil. 11. Cook at 200°C for 3 minutes, flip, spray with oil, and cook for 3 more minutes. 12. Dust with the icing sugar before serving.
Per Serving: Calories 419; Fat 3.23g; Sodium 416 mg; Carbs 92.61g; Fibre 1.4g; Sugar 59.79g; Protein 5.97 g

Quick and Easy Apple Pie Egg Rolls

Prep Time: 10 **minutes** | **Cook Time:** 8 minutes | **Serves:** 6

Oil, for spraying
1 (525g) can apple pie filling
1 tablespoon plain flour
½ teaspoon lemon juice
¼ teaspoon ground nutmeg
¼ teaspoon ground cinnamon
6 egg roll wrappers

1. Turn on the air fryer and preheat it to 205°C. Line the air fryer basket with parchment and sprinkle with oil. 2. Mix together the pie filling, flour, lemon juice, nutmeg, and cinnamon in a bowl. 3. Lay out the egg roll wrappers on a work surface and spoon a dollop of pie filling in the centre of each. 4. Fill a small bowl with water. Dip your finger in the water and, working one at a time, moisten the edges of the wrappers. Fold the wrapper like an envelope: First fold one corner into the centre. Fold each side corner in, and then fold over the remaining corner, making sure each corner overlaps a bit and the moistened edges stay closed. Use additional water and your fingers to seal any open edges. 5. Place the rolls in the air fryer basket and spray liberally with oil. 6. Cook for 4 minutes, flip, spray with oil, and cook for 4 more minutes.
Per Serving: Calories 198; Fat 0.63g; Sodium 230 mg; Carbs 45.59g; Fibre 1.7g; Sugar 13.71g; Protein 3.38g

Great Funnel Cake

Prep Time: 10 **minutes** | **Cook Time:** 5 minutes | **Serves:** 4

Oil, for spraying
125g self-rising flour, plus more for dusting
245g fat-free vanilla Greek yogurt
½ teaspoon ground cinnamon
30g confectioners' sugar

1. Turn on the air fryer and preheat it to 190°C. Line the air fryer basket with parchment and sprinkle with oil. 2. Mix together the flour, yogurt, and cinnamon in a bowl until the mixture forms a ball. 3. Place the dough on a lightly floured work surface and knead for about 2 minutes. 4. Cut the dough into 4 equal pieces, then cut each of those into 6 pieces. 5.Roll the pieces into 20 – 25 cmlong ropes. Loosely mound the ropes into 4 piles of 6 ropes. 6.Place the dough piles in the air fryer basket and spray liberally with oil. 7.Cook for 5 minutes. 8.Dust with the icing' sugar before serving.

Per Serving: Calories 148; Fat 1.44g; Sodium 377 mg; Carbs 30.12g; Fibre 1g; Sugar 6.58g; Protein 3.27 g

Perfect Grilled Peaches

Prep Time: 5 **minutes** | **Cook Time:** 10 minutes | **Serves:** 4

Oil, for spraying
15g digestive biscuit cracker crumbs
55g light brown sugar
8 tablespoons unsalted butter, cubed
¼ teaspoon cinnamon
2 peaches, pitted and cut into quarters
4 scoops vanilla ice cream

1.Line the air fryer basket with parchment and sprinkle with oil. 2. Mix together the digestive biscuit crumbs, brown sugar, butter, and cinnamon with a fork until crumbly in a bowl. 3. Place the peach wedges in the air fryer basket, skin-side up. 4. Cook at 175°C for 5 minutes, flip, and sprinkle with a spoonful of the graham cracker mixture. Cook for 5 more minutes. 5.Top with a scoop of vanilla ice cream and any remaining crumble mixture. Serve immediately.

Per Serving: Calories 472; Fat 31.54g; Sodium 127mg; Carbs 42.91g; Fibre 1.7g; Sugar 37.84g; Protein 6.01g

Classic Shortbread Sticks

Prep Time: 10 **minutes** | **Cook Time:** 10 minutes | **Serves:** 4

Oil, for spraying
250g self-rising flour
170g unsalted butter, cubed
40g icing sugar

1. Line the air fryer basket with parchment and sprinkle with oil. 2. Mix together the flour, butter, and icing sugar with your hands until it resembles thick bread crumbs in a bowl. Continue to knead until the mixture forms a dough ball. 3. On a work surface, roll out the dough until it is ½ to 1 cm thick. 4. Cut the dough into 8 to 10 cm long sticks. 5. Place the sticks in the air fryer basket. 6. Cook the sticks at 360 °F/ 180°C for 10 minutes. If you want the shortbread to be more golden brown, cook for 2 more minutes. Let cool completely on the parchment before serving.

Per Serving: Calories 506; Fat 24.87g; Sodium 761mg; Carbs 63.1g; Fibre 1.7g; Sugar 16.52g; Protein 7.57g

Irresistible Churro Bites

Prep Time: 5 minutes | **Cook Time:** 6 minutes | **Serves:** 12

Oil, for spraying
1 (430g) package frozen puffed pastry, thawed
200g granulated sugar
1 tablespoon ground cinnamon
60g icing sugar
1 tablespoon milk

1. Turn on the air fryer and preheat it to 205°C. Line the air fryer basket with parchment and sprinkle with oil. 2.Unfold the puff pastry onto a clean work surface. Using a sharp knife, cut the dough into 36 bite-size pieces. 3. Place the dough pieces in one layer in the air fryer basket, taking care not to let the pieces touch or overlap. 4. Cook for 3 minutes, flip, and cook for 3 more minutes. 5. Mix together the granulated sugar and cinnamon in a bowl. 6. Whisk together the icing sugar and milk in a bowl. 7.Dredge the bites in the cinnamon-sugar mixture until evenly coated. 8. Serve with the icing on the side for dipping.
Per Serving: Calories 279; Fat 15.8g; Sodium 104mg; Carbs 31.7g; Fibre 1g; Sugar 12.61g; Protein 3.08g

Easy and Delicious Apple Fries

Prep Time: 10 minutes | **Cook Time:** 7 minutes | **Serves:** 8

Oil, for spraying
125g plain flour
3 large eggs, beaten
60g digestive biscuits
50g sugar
1 teaspoon ground cinnamon
3 large Gala apples, peeled, cored, and cut into wedges
340g caramel sauce, warmed

1. Turn on the air fryer and preheat it to 195°C. Line the air fryer basket with parchment and sprinkle with oil. 2. Place the flour and beaten eggs in divide bowls and set aside. Mix together the digestive biscuit crumbs, sugar, and cinnamon in a bowl. 3. Working one at a time, coat the apple wedges in the flour, dip in the egg, and dredge in the digestive biscuit mix until evenly coated. 4. Place the apples in the air fryer basket, taking care not to overlap, and sprinkle with oil. 5. Cook for 5 minutes, flip, spray with oil, and cook for 2 more minutes. 6.Drizzle the caramel sauce over the top.
Per Serving: Calories 156; Fat 2.76g; Sodium242 mg; Carbs 29.43g; Fibre 3g; Sugar 12.67g; Protein 3.45g

Easy S'more

Prep Time: 5 minutes | **Cook Time:** 30 seconds | **Serves:** 4.

Oil, for spraying
8 digestive biscuits
2 (40g) chocolate bars
4 large marshmallows

1.Line the air fryer basket with parchment and sprinkle with oil. 2.Place 4 graham cracker squares in the air fryer basket. 3. Break the chocolate bars in half and place 1 piece on top of each disgestive biscuit. Top with 1 marshmallow. 4. Cook them at 185°C for 30 seconds. 5.Top with the remaining digestive biscuit, and enjoy.
Per Serving: Calories 247; Fat 13.64g; Sodium 78mg; Carbs 28.49g; Fibre 3.4g; Sugar 13.69g; Protein 3.14g

Delicious Meringue Cookies

Prep Time: 15 minutes | **Cook Time:** 90 minutes | **Serves:** 10

Oil, for spraying
4 large egg whites
190g sugar
Pinch cream of tartar

1. Turn on the air fryer and preheat it to 60°C. Line the air fryer basket with parchment and sprinkle with oil. 2. Whisk together the egg whites and sugar in a bowl. Fill a small saucepan halfway with water, place it over medium heat, and bring to a light simmer. Place the bowl with the egg whites on the saucepan, making sure the bottom of the bowl does not touch the water. Whisk the mixture until the sugar is dissolved. 3. Transfer the mixture to a large bowl and add the cream of tartar. Using an electric mixer, beat the mixture on high until it is glossy and stiff peaks form. Transfer the mixture to a piping bag or a zip-top plastic bag with a corner cut off. 4. Pipe rounds into the air fryer basket. 5. Cook for 1 hour 30 minutes. 6. Turn off the air fryer and let the meringues cool completely inside. The residual heat will continue to dry them out.
Per Serving: Calories 47; Fat 0.02g; Sodium 22mg; Carbs 10.26g; Fibre 0g; Sugar 9.87g; Protein 1.44g

Great Chocolate-Stuffed Wontons

Prep Time: 10 minutes | **Cook Time:** 10 minutes | **Serves:** 12

Oil, for spraying
200g cream cheese
95g granulated sugar
20g unsweetened cocoa powder
1 teaspoon almond extract
24 wonton wrappers
15g icing sugar

1. Line the air fryer basket with parchment and sprinkle with oil. 2. Mix together the cream cheese, granulated sugar, cocoa powder, and almond extract until creamy in a bowl. 3. Lay the wonton wrappers on a work surface and place 1 tablespoon of the chocolate filling in the centre of each one. 4. Fill a small bowl with water. Dip your finger in the water and moisten the outer edges of each wrapper. Fold the wonton in half, corner to corner, and pinch the edges together to seal. 5. Place the wontons in the air fryer basket and spray with oil. 6. Cook at 175°C for 5 minutes, shake, spray with oil, and cook for 5 more minutes. 7. Dust with the icing sugar before serving.
Per Serving: Calories 271; Fat 6.65g; Sodium 449mg; Carbs 45.02g; Fibre 1.7g; Sugar 6.81g; Protein 7.96 g

Quick and Easy Chocolate Mug Cake

Prep Time: 2 minutes | **Cook Time:** 13 minutes | **Serve:** 1

Oil, for spraying
6 tablespoons chocolate cake mix
2 tablespoons unsweetened applesauce
1 tablespoon water

1. Line the air fryer basket with parchment and sprinkle with oil. 2. Whisk together the cake mix, applesauce, and water until smooth in a mug. 3. Place the mug in the air fryer basket. 4. Cook the cake at 175°C for 12 to 13 minutes. 5. Let the cakes cool for a few minutes before serving.
Per Serving: Calories 137; Fat 7.76g; Sodium 59 mg; Carbs 15.32g; Fibre 0.7g; Sugar 2.86g; Protein 3.28g

Chocolate Pavlova

Prep Time: 15 minutes | **Cook Time:** 90 minutes | **Serves:** 2

For Pavlova
2 large egg whites
¼ teaspoon cream of tartar
10g powdered sweetener
1 tablespoon unsweetened cocoa powder
1 teaspoon instant espresso powder
½ teaspoon apple cider vinegar
½ teaspoon vanilla extract

For Topping
60g heavy whipping cream
2 tablespoons powdered sweetener
1 tablespoon sour cream
1 teaspoon instant espresso powder
25g dark chocolate

1. Cut a piece of parchment paper to size of a grill pan. Draw a 15 cm circle on paper. Flip paper, ink side down, onto grill pan. 2. To make Pavlova: In a medium metal bowl, beat egg whites with an immersion blender on high. Add cream of tartar, then add sweetener, 1 tablespoon at a time, and blend until stiff peaks form. 3. Fold in cocoa powder and espresso powder. Blend in apple cider vinegar and vanilla. 4. Preheat air fryer at 105°C for 5 minutes. 5. Spoon or pipe egg whites over parchment paper circle, creating higher edges around perimeter, like a pie crust. There should be a divot in the centre.6. Add grill pan to air fryer and cook for 60 minutes. 7. Turn off heat, and let pavlova stay in air fryer an additional 30 minutes. 8. Remove grill pan from air fryer and gently peel off parchment paper from bottom of pavlova. Transfer to a large plate. 9. To make Topping: Whisk together whipping cream and sweetener in a small bowl. Fold in sour cream and espresso powder. 10. Fill pavlova with whipped cream. Using a vegetable peeler, shave chocolate into curls over pavlova.

Per Serving: Calories 220; Fat 15.47g; Sodium 74mg; Carbs 22.27g; Fibre8.8g; Sugar 4.76g; Protein 9.61g

Tasty Banana Bread Muffins

Prep Time: 10 minutes | **Cook Time:** 18 minutes | **Serves:** 6

2 ripe bananas
2 tablespoons ground flaxseed
60ml unsweetened plant-based milk
1 tablespoon apple cider vinegar
1 tablespoon vanilla extract
½ teaspoon ground cinnamon
2 tablespoons pure maple syrup
60g oat flour
½ teaspoon baking soda
3 tablespoons natural peanut butter

1. Use a fork to mash the bananas in a medium bowl, leaving some small chunks intact for texture; add the flaxseed, plant-based milk, apple cider vinegar, vanilla, cinnamon, and maple syrup to the bowl, and mix them until well combined. Then, add the oat flour and baking soda and mix again. 2. Spoon the batter into 6 cupcake molds. Then, place 1½ teaspoons peanut butter on top of each muffin. Swirl it around a little bit so that it sticks.3. Place the muffins in the air fryer basket, and bake them in the air fryer at 160°C for 18 minutes. Let them cool before enjoying.

Per Serving: Calories 141; Fat 4.02g; Sodium 234mg; Carbs 23.08g; Fibre 2.8g; Sugar 11.3g; Protein 3.24 g

Irresistible Raspberry Pavlova with Orange Cream

Prep Time: 15 minutes | **Cook Time:** 90 minutes | **Serves:** 2

For Pavlova
2 large egg whites
¼ teaspoon cream of tartar
10g powdered sweetener
½ teaspoon pulp-free orange juice
½ teaspoon vanilla extract

For Topping
80g heavy whipping cream
1 teaspoon fresh orange juice
¼ teaspoon orange zest
2 tablespoons powdered sweetener
125g fresh raspberries

1. Cut a piece of parchment paper to the size of a grill pan. Draw a 15 cm circle on paper. Flip paper, ink side down, onto grill pan. 2. To make Pavlova: In a medium metal bowl, beat egg whites with a hand held blender on high. Add cream of tartar, then add sweetener, 1 tablespoon at a time, until stiff peaks form. Add orange juice and vanilla and blend. 3. Preheat air fryer at 105°C for 5 minutes. 4. Spoon or pipe egg whites over parchment paper circle, creating higher edges around perimeter, like a pie crust. There should be a divot in the centre. 5. Add grill pan to air fryer and cook 60 minutes. 6. Turn off heat, and let pavlova sit in air fryer an additional 30 minutes. 7. Remove grill pan from air fryer and gently peel off parchment paper from bottom of pavlova. Transfer to a large plate. 8. To make Topping: Whisk together whipping cream, orange juice, orange zest, and sweetener until creamy in a bowl. 9. Fill pavlova with whipped cream and top with raspberries, and enjoy.

Per Serving: Calories 220; Fat 15.47g; Sodium 74mg; Carbs 22.27g; Fibre8.8g; Sugar 4.76g; Protein9.61g

Irresistible Carrot Cake Muffins

Prep Time: 10 minutes | **Cook Time:** 15 minutes | **Serves:** 6

110g grated carrot
55g chopped pineapple
35g raisins
2 tablespoons pure maple syrup
80ml unsweetened plant-based milk
125g oat flour
1 teaspoon ground cinnamon
½ teaspoon ground ginger
1 teaspoon baking powder
½ teaspoon baking soda
40g chopped walnuts

1. Mix together the carrot, pineapple, raisins, maple syrup, and plant-based milk in a bowl. Then add the oat flour, cinnamon, ginger, baking powder, and baking soda and mix again until just combined.2. Divide the batter evenly among 6 cupcake molds. Then sprinkle the chopped walnuts evenly over each muffin. Lightly press the walnuts into the batter so they are partially submerged.3. Bake them at 175°C for 15 minutes. Let the muffins cool completely before enjoying.

Per Serving: Calories 141; Fat 4.79g; Sodium 129mg; Carbs 21.87g; Fibre 2.3g; Sugar 7.84g; Protein 3.92 g

Simple Blueberry Hand Pies

Prep Time: 15 minutes | **Cook Time:** 10 minutes | **Serves:** 12

Oil, for spraying
250g plain flour
¼ teaspoon baking soda
¼ teaspoon salt
120ml vegetable oil
80ml buttermilk
1 (525g) can blueberry pie filling
1 large egg, beaten
120g icing sugar
2 tablespoons milk

1. Line the air fryer basket with parchment and sprinkle with oil. 2. Mix together the flour, baking soda, and salt in a bowl. Add the vegetable oil and buttermilk and mix together until the mixture forms a ball. 3. Roll out the dough on a work surface until it is about ½ cm thick. Using a 10 cm biscuit cutter, cut the dough into 12 circles. 4. Spoon a dollop of pie filling in the centre of each dough circle. 5. Fill a small bowl with water. Wet the edges of the dough with water, then fold the dough in half and press the edges with a fork to seal it closed. 6. Brush the pies with the egg. Using a fork, poke small holes in the top of each pie. 7. Place the pies in the air fryer basket, taking care not to overlap, and sprinkle oil over them. 8. Cook the pies at 175°C for 10 minutes. Let cool completely. 9. Whisk together the icing sugar and milk and set aside in a bowl. 10. Have a piece of parchment paper or a large plate nearby. Dip the pies in the glaze mixture, turning to coat both sides. 11. Use a fork to lift them out of the bowl and to help shake off any excess. Place them on the parchment and let the glaze dry before serving.
Per Serving: Calories 245; Fat 9.85g; Sodium 114mg; Carbs37.66g; Fibre 11g; Sugar 15.51g; Protein 2.73g

Delicious Berry Cheese Cake

Prep Time: 5 minutes | **Cook Time:** 10 minutes | **Serves:** 4

Oil, for spraying
200g cream cheese
6 tablespoons sugar
1 tablespoon sour cream
1 large egg
½ teaspoon vanilla extract
¼ teaspoon lemon juice
70g fresh mixed berries

1.Turn on the air fryer and preheat it to 175°C. Line the air fryer basket with parchment and sprinkle with oil. 2. Add the cream cheese, sugar, sour cream, egg, vanilla, and lemon juice to a blender, and blend them until smooth. Pour the mixture into a 10 cm spring form pan. 3. Place the pan in the air fryer basket. 4. Cook the mixture for 8 to 10 minutes. 5.Refrigerate the cheesecake in the pan for at least 2 hours. 6.Release the sides from the spring form pan, top the cheesecake with the mixed berries,.
Per Serving: Calories 306; Fat 20.36g; Sodium 307mg; Carbs 26.08g; Fibre 0.5g; Sugar 20.25g; Protein 5.56g

Low-carb Nutty Chocolate Cheesecake

Prep Time: 10 minutes | **Cook Time:** 24 minutes | **Serves:** 6

110g ground pecans (pecan meal)
3 tablespoons butter, melted
3 tablespoons granular sweetener
2 teaspoons instant espresso powder
300g cream cheese, room temperature
2 tablespoons sour cream
2 large eggs
20g unsweetened cocoa
10g powdered sweetener
1 teaspoon vanilla extract
⅛ teaspoon salt
40g mini sugar-free chocolate chips
30g pecan pieces

1. Preheat air fryer at 205°C for 3 minutes. 2. Combine ground pecans, butter, granular sweetener, and espresso powder in a medium bowl. Press mixture into an ungreased 18 cm spring-form pan. 3. Place pan in air fryer basket and bake for 5 minutes. Remove from air fryer basket and allow to cool for 15 minutes. 4. In a divide medium bowl, combine cream cheese, sour cream, eggs, unsweetened cocoa, powdered sweetener, vanilla, and salt until smooth. Spoon mixture over crust. Cover with aluminum foil. 5. Place spring-form pan back into air fryer basket and cook 14 minutes. 6. Remove aluminum foil and cook for an additional 5 minutes at 175°C. 7. Remove cheesecake from air fryer basket. Garnish with chocolate chips and pecan pieces. 8. Cover cheesecake and refrigerate at least 2 hours to allow it to set. Once set, release sides of pan.
Per Serving: Calories 431; Fat 41.57g; Sodium 479 mg; Carbs 10.99g; Fibre 4.2g; Sugar 3.08g; Protein 10.38g

Flavourful Chocolate Surprise Cookies

Prep Time: 15 minutes | **Cook Time:** 8 minutes | **Serves:** 5

1 tablespoon ground flaxseed
3 tablespoons water
1 teaspoon vanilla extract
1 teaspoon apple cider vinegar
85g natural peanut butter
110g honey
20g cacao powder
¼ teaspoon baking soda

1. Combine the flaxseed, water, vanilla, and apple cider vinegar in a bowl. Let sit for 5 minutes. 2. Add the peanut butter and honey to the bowl, and mix again. Sprinkle in the cacao powder and baking soda and mix until well combined. The mixture should be quite thick. 3. Line the air fryer basket or rack with parchment paper. Scoop the dough into 2-tablespoon balls and place them in the air fryer, leaving some space between each. 4. Bake the dough at 150°C for 8 minutes. 5. Use a fork to flatten each cookie slightly while they're still hot. 6. Let the cookies cool completely before taking them off the parchment paper, as they will still firm and crisp up a bit as they cool.
Per Serving: Calories 167; Fat 7.96g; Sodium 171mg; Carbs 21.08g; Fibre 2.9g; Sugar 11.86g; Protein 6.09g

Fancy Chocolate Lava Cakes

Prep Time: 7 minutes | **Cook Time:** 12 minutes | **Serves:** 4

Oil, for greasing
110g semisweet chocolate chips
8 tablespoons unsalted butter, cubed
60g icing sugar
2 large eggs plus 2 large egg yolks, at room temperature
1 teaspoon vanilla extract
6 tablespoons plain flour
4 scoops vanilla ice cream, for serving
Chocolate syrup, for serving

1. Preheat the air fryer to 190°C. Grease 4 ramekins and set aside. 2. In a microwave-safe bowl, combine the chocolate chips and butter, and microwave on high for 30 to 45 seconds. 3. Add the icing sugar, eggs, egg yolks, and vanilla and whisk to combine. Fold in the flour. 4. Divide the batter evenly among the ramekins and place them into the air fryer. 5. Cook for 10 to 12 minutes. 6. Let stand for 5 minutes. Invert the ramekins onto individual plates, top with ice cream and a drizzle of chocolate syrup, then serve.
Per Serving: Calories 616; Fat 29.86g; Sodium 127 mg; Carbs 86.94g; Fibre 2.3g; Sugar 57.8g; Protein7.91 g

Perfect Overload Dessert Pizza

Prep Time: 8 minutes | **Cook Time:** 13 minutes | **Serves:** 4

Oil, for greasing
4 tablespoons unsalted butter, at room temperature
50g granulated sugar
55g packed light brown sugar
½ large egg
½ teaspoon vanilla extract
95g plain flour
¼ teaspoon baking soda
⅛ teaspoon salt
85g semisweet chocolate chips
120g chopped chocolate bars and candies

1. Turn on the air fryer and preheat it to 175°C. Grease a 15 or 18 cm round metal cake pan, depending on the size of your air fryer. 2. In a large bowl, beat the butter, granulated sugar, and brown sugar with an electric mixer until creamy. Add the egg and vanilla and beat until combined. 3. Add the flour, baking soda, and salt and beat until smooth. Fold in the chocolate chips. 4. Press the dough into the prepared pan. 5. Cook the dough for 9 to 11 minutes until the edges are lightly browned; top with the chopped candy, and cook for 1 to 2 minutes more until lightly melted. .6. Serve and enjoy.
Per Serving: Calories 379; Fat 19.87g; Sodium 231mg; Carbs 47.76g; Fibre 3.4g; Sugar 13.12g; Protein 6g

Delicious Pumpkin Mug Cake

Prep Time: 5 minutes | **Cook Time:** 25 minutes | **Serve:** 1

1 large egg
1 tablespoon coconut flour
1 tablespoon almond flour
2 tablespoons heavy whipping cream
2 tablespoons granular sweetener
2 teaspoons pumpkin pie spice
¼ teaspoon maple extract
¼ teaspoon baking powder
2 tablespoons chopped walnuts
⅛ teaspoon salt

1. Preheat air fryer at 150°C for 3 minutes. 2. Whisk egg together with remaining ingredients in a bowl. 3. Pour batter into a 10 cm ramekin greased with cooking spray. 4. Place ramekin in air fryer basket and cook for 25 minutes. 5. Remove ramekin from air fryer basket and let sit for 5 minutes.
Per Serving: Calories 366; Fat 31.66g; Sodium 829mg; Carbs 9.07g; Fibre 1.9g; Sugar 2.78g; Protein 15.5g

Delightful Almond Delights

Prep Time: 10 minutes | **Cook Time:** 18 minutes | **Serves:** 4

1 ripe banana
1 tablespoon almond extract
½ teaspoon ground cinnamon
2 tablespoons coconut sugar
95g almond flour
¼ teaspoon baking soda
8 raw almonds

1. Mash the banana in a medium bowl; add the almond extract, cinnamon, and coconut sugar and mix until well combined. Add the almond flour and baking soda to the bowl and mix again. 2. Line the air fryer basket or rack with parchment paper. Divide the dough into 8 equal balls and flatten each ball to 1 cm thick on the parchment paper. Press 1 almond into the centre of each cookie. 3. Bake the cookies at 150°C for 12 minutes. Then, flip the cookies over and bake for an additional 6 minutes. 4. Let cool slightly before enjoying.
Per Serving: Calories 60; Fat 1.6g; Sodium 83mg; Carbs 11.64g; Fibre 1.3g; Sugar 7.66g; Protein 0.97 g

Conclusion

The air fryer is arguably the most versatile and advanced cooking appliance in the world. These devices have a large capacity and are the perfect cooking companion for you and your family.
The air fryer has numerous cooking functions; you can make practically anything. This cookbook has many air-frying recipes with step-by-step instructions, easy-to-find ingredients, precise prep/cook time, and serving suggestions.
Air fryers come with practical accessories that enable you to cook any meal you desire. I recommend this appliance because it cooks food in very little time, the cleaning process is straightforward, and the unit is safe to use.
My cookbook has many delicious air-frying recipes, helping you to prepare and cook food for yourself, family and friends. It's so easy to use. Place food in the basket or tray, adjust the temperature and cooking time, and enjoy more time with your loved ones.
I hope you enjoy using this cookbook and that it serves you well for years to come. Thank you for bringing it into your home.

Appendix 1 Measurement Conversion Chart

VOLUME EQUIVALENTS (LIQUID)

US STANDARD	US STANDARD (OUNCES)	METRIC (APPROXIMATE)
2 tablespoons	1 fl.oz	30 mL
¼ cup	2 fl.oz	60 mL
½ cup	4 fl.oz	120 mL
1 cup	8 fl.oz	240 mL
1½ cup	12 fl.oz	355 mL
2 cups or 1 pint	16 fl.oz	475 mL
4 cups or 1 quart	32 fl.oz	1 L
1 gallon	128 fl.oz	4 L

VOLUME EQUIVALENTS (DRY)

US STANDARD	METRIC (APPROXIMATE)
⅛ teaspoon	0.5 mL
¼ teaspoon	1 mL
½ teaspoon	2 mL
¾ teaspoon	4 mL
1 teaspoon	5 mL
1 tablespoon	15 mL
¼ cup	59 mL
½ cup	118 mL
¾ cup	177 mL
1 cup	235 mL
2 cups	475 mL
3 cups	700 mL
4 cups	1 L

TEMPERATURES EQUIVALENTS

FAHRENHEIT(F)	CELSIUS (C) (APPROXIMATE)
225 °F	107 °C
250 °F	120 °C
275 °F	135 °C
300 °F	150 °C
325 °F	160 °C
350 °F	180 °C
375 °F	190 °C
400 °F	205 °C
425 °F	220 °C
450 °F	235 °C
475 °F	245 °C
500 °F	260 °C

WEIGHT EQUIVALENTS

US STANDARD	METRIC (APPROXINATE)
1 ounce	28 g
2 ounces	57 g
5 ounces	142 g
10 ounces	284 g
15 ounces	425 g
16 ounces (1 pound)	455 g
1.5 pounds	680 g
2 pounds	907 g

Appendix 2 Air Fryer Cooking Chart

vegetables	Temp (°F)	Time (min)	Meat	Temp (°F)	Time (min)
Asparagus (1-inch slices)	400	5	Bacon	400	5 to 7
Beets (sliced)	350	25	Beef Eye Round Roast (4 lbs.)	390	50 to 60
Beets (whole)	400	40	Burger (4 oz.)	370	16 to 20
Bell Peppers (sliced)	350	13	Chicken Breasts, bone-in (1.25 lbs.)	370	25
Broccoli	400	6	Chicken Breasts, boneless (4 oz.)	380	12
Brussels Sprouts (halved)	380	15	Chicken Drumsticks (2.5 lbs.)	370	20
Carrots (½-inch slices)	380	15	Chicken Thighs, bone-in (2 lbs.)	380	22
Cauliflower (florets)	400	12	Chicken Thighs, boneless (1.5 lbs.)	380	18 to 20
Eggplant (1½-inch cubes)	400	15	Chicken Legs, bone-in (1.75 lbs.)	380	30
Fennel (quartered)	370	15	Chicken Wings (2 lbs.)	400	12
Mushrooms (¼-inch slices)	400	5	Flank Steak (1.5 lbs.)	400	12
Onion (pearl)	400	10	Game Hen (halved, 2 lbs.)	390	20
Parsnips (½-inch chunks)	380	5	Loin (2 lbs.)	360	55
Peppers (1-inch chunks)	400	15	London Broil (2 lbs.)	400	20 to 28
Potatoes (baked, whole)	400	40	Meatballs (3-inch)	380	10
Squash (½-inch chunks)	400	12	Rack of Lamb (1.5-2 lbs.)	380	22
Tomatoes (cherry)	400	4	Sausages	380	15
Zucchni (½-inch sticks)	400	12	Whole Chicken (6.5 lbs.)	360	75

Fish and Seafood			Frozen Foods		
Calamari (8 oz.)	400	4	Onion Rings (12 oz.)	400	8
Fish Fillet (1-inch, 8 oz.)	400	10	Thin French Fries (20 oz.)	400	14
Salmon Fillet (6 oz.)	380	12	Thick French Fries (17 oz.)	400	18
Tuna Steak	400	7 to 10	Pot Sticks (10 oz.)	400	8
Scallops	400	5 to 7	Fish Sticks (10 oz.)	400	10
Shrimp	400	5	Fish Fillets (½-inch, 10 oz.)	400	14

Appendix 3 Recipes Index

"Fried" Chicken 55

A
Air Fried Worcestershire Pork Belly 75
Air Fryer Baby Back Ribs 75
Air-Fryer Avocado Fries 85
Air-Fryer Barbecue Turnip Chips 92
Air-Fryer Jalapeño Poppers 84
Almond and Mozzarella Cheese Pizza Rolls 92
Apricot-Glazed Turkey Tenderloin 60
Asparagus and Pepper Strata Sandwich 15
Avocado and Egg Burrito 15

B
Bacon and Cheese Burger Casserole 73
Bacon Cheeseburger Dip 94
Bacon Jalapeño Cheese Bread 87
Bacon, Egg, and Cheddar Cheese Roll Ups 24
Bacon-Wrapped Brie 90
Bacon-Wrapped Onion Rings 81
Balsamic Chicken and Veggies 63
Beef and Chorizo Burger 72
Black Pepper and Cauliflower Avocado Toast 18
Black Pepper Chicken with Celery 66
Breaded Chicken Strips 65
Breakfast Bake with Loaded Cauliflower 22
Breakfast Sausage and Cheese Balls 18
Breakfast Sausage Stuffed with Poblanos 21
Broccoli with Twice-baked Potatoes 36
Butter Flaky Biscuits 35
Butter Fried Cabbage 26
Butter Pork Chops 67

C
Cajun Pepper & Chicken Kebabs 53
Cajun Thyme Chicken Tenders 56
California Deviled Eggs 93
Carrot and Golden Raisin Muffins 14
Cheddar Cheese and Buffalo Egg Cups 17
Cheddar Cheesy Cauliflower Hash Browns 22
Cheddar Cheesy Pepper Eggs 18
Cheddar Jalapeño Popper Hasselback Chicken 56
Cheddar Stuffed Peppers 62

Cheese and Spinach Steak Rolls 73
Cheese-Stuffed Steak Burgers 68
Chicken Sausages with Black Pepper 16
Chicken Taquitos 59
Chicken Wraps 64
Chicken-Avocado Enchiladas 57
Chocolate Pavlova 99
Cinnamon Crunchy Granola 15
Classic Crab Cakes 40
Classic Parmesan French Fries 34
Classic Pulled Pork 75
Classic Shortbread Sticks 96
Courgette Chips 82
Cranberry and Bran Flake Muffins 16
Crave-worthy Chicken Courgette Boats 33
Creamy Chicken Corden Bleu Casserole 56
Crisp Brussels Sprouts 34
Crisp Flounder au Gratin 47
Crispy Baby Potatoes 26
Crispy Chicken TendersCrispy Chicken Tender 59
Crispy Chicken Wings 86
Crispy Ham Egg Cups 20
Crispy Okra 28
Crispy Roasted Broccoli 36
Crispy Stir-fried Beef and Broccoli 78
Crispy Sweet Potato Fries 35
Crumbled Sausage and Scrambled Egg 23
Crunchy Roasted Edamame 31
Crunchy Tortilla Chips 82
Crusted Buttery Beef Tenderloin 74
Crusted Chicken 55

D
Delicate Crab Ratatouille 52
Delicate Steamed Tuna 45
Delicious Berry Cheese Cake 101
Delicious Butternut Squash 30
Delicious Catfish Bites 43
Delicious Deviled Eggs 93
Delicious Meringue Cookies 98
Delicious Prawns Kebabs 41
Delicious Pumpkin Mug Cake 104
Delicious Street Corn 28
Delightful Almond Delights 104
Delightful Crispy Fried Calamari 43
Dijon Roasted Turkey Breast 65
Distinct Cajun Prawns 51

Dried Fruit Beignets with Brown Sugar 24

E

Easy and Delicious Apple Fries 97
Easy and Delicious Coriander Butter Baked Mahi Mahi 44
Easy Courgette Chips 33
Easy French Mussels 46
Easy Garlic Pesto Scallops 44
Easy S'more 97
Easy Tuna Veggie Stir-Fry 45
Efficient Cod Piccata with Roasted Potatoes 49

F

Fabulous Tuna Melt 38
Fajita Flank Steak Rolls 76
Family Favorite Thai-style Prawns Stir-fry 43
Fancy Chocolate Lava Cakes 103
Flavourful Chocolate Surprise Cookies 102
Flavourful Hot Crab Dip 41
Fluffy Cheese Bread 81
Fresh Garlic-Dill Salmon with Tomatoes & Green Beans 49
Fried Bacon-Wrapped Jalapeño Poppers 86
Fried Black Bean Corn Dip 82
Fried Cinnamon and Sugar Peaches 80
Fried Cinnamon Apple Chips 88
Fried Edamame 80
Fried Parmesan Chicken Wings 87
Fried Salmon and Brown Rice Frittata 25

G

Golden Garlic Knots 29
Gorgeous Honey-Balsamic Salmon 41
Great Chocolate-Stuffed Wontons 98
Great Coconut Prawns with Orange Sauce 38
Great Cod with Creamy Mustard Sauce 47
Great Funnel Cake 96
Great Herbed Salmon 42
Green Tomatoes 37
Green Veggie Trio 33

H

Healthy Fried Tilapia 39
Healthy Kale Chips 28

I

Irresistible Carrot Cake Muffins 100
Irresistible Carrots 27
Irresistible Chili-Lime Tilapia 44
Irresistible Churro Bites 97
Irresistible Raspberry Pavlova with Orange Cream 100
Italian Beef Meatballs 71
Italian Mozzarella Sticklets 83
Italian Pepperoni Pizza Bread 90
Italian Salsa Verde 91

J

Jalapeño Egg Cups 16
Jalapeño Popper 91
Juicy Baked Pork Chops 73
Juicy Teriyaki Salmon 51

L

Lasagna Casserole 74
Lemon Pepper Chicken Drumsticks 54
Lemon-Herb Tuna Steaks 48
Lime Chicken Thighs 58
London Steak 71
Low-carb Nutty Chocolate Cheesecake 102

M

Marinated Ribeye Steak 69
Marinated Steak Kebabs 68
Mayo Chicken 57
Mexican Fried Potato Skins 94
Mexican Sheet Pan Chicken Supper 60
Mexican Shredded Beef 70
Milk and Pumpkin Donut Holes 14
Mini Sweet Pepper Bacon Poppers 81
Mozzarella Cheese Sticks 88
Mozzarella Chicken Pizza Crust 54
Mozzarella Corn Dogs Mozzarella 68
Mozzarella-Stuffed Buffalo Meatballs 88
Mozzarella-Stuffed Meatloaf 79

P

Parmesan Cermini Mushrooms 30
Parmesan Veggie Frittata 25
Parmesan-crumb Chicken 63
Parmesan-Crusted Pork Chops 69
Pepperoni and Chicken Pizza Bake 57
Peppers with Garlic 37
Perfect Beignets 95
Perfect Grilled Peaches 96
Perfect Haddock Fish Fingers 50
Perfect Lemon Mahi-mahi 39
Perfect Lemon Pepper Prawns 39
Perfect Overload Dessert Pizza 103
Perfect Potato Wedges 29

Perfect Seafood Tacos 42
Pineapple Chicken Kebabs 53
Popular Buffalo Cauliflower 32
Popular Fried Garlic Prawns 46
Pork Chops Stuffed with Bacon and Cheese 69
Pork Meatballs 70
Pork Tenderloin with Mustard 67
Prosciutto-Wrapped Asparagus 86

Q

Quick and Easy Apple Pie Egg Rolls 95
Quick and Easy Chocolate Mug Cake 98
Quick Bacon Strips 19
Quick Corn Casserole 29
Quick Scallops and Spring Veggies 45

R

Roast Beef 71
Roasted Jack-O'-Lantern Seeds with black pepper 84

S

Satisfying Parmesan Perch 50
Savory Latin American-style Pastries 76
Savory Sesame Chicken Tenders 61
Scalloped Potato Slices 32
Scrambled Eggs with Cheddar Cheese 22
Sesame Carrots 32
Simple Air Fryer "Hard-Boiled" Eggs 21
Simple Baked Brie with Orange Marmalade and Spiced Walnuts 85
Simple Blueberry Hand Pies 101
Simple Bone Marrow Butter 83
Simple Chicken Fajitas 55
Simple Five Spice Crunchy Edamame 81
Simple French Toast Sticks 20
Simple Mini Meatloaf 79
Simple Mozzarella Pizza Crust 89
Simple Pumpkin Spice Muffins 17
Simple Snapper Scampi 52
Simple Turkey Tenderloin 59
Smoky Roasted Almonds 90
Sophisticated Fish Sticks 40
Southern-style Breaded Pork Chops 74
Spanish Quick Paella 42
Spice-Rubbed Pork Loin 72
Spicy Air-Fryer Sunflower Seeds 84
Spicy Fried Buffalo Chicken Dip 87
Spicy Fried Chickpeas 80
Spicy Pork Spare Ribs 70

Spinach and Feta-Stuffed Chicken Breast 66
Spinach Artichoke Dip 89
Spinach, Cheese and Chicken Meatballs 64
Stuffed Chicken Breast 54
Stuffed Peppers 78
Super-Fast Green Bean Fries 27
Sweet Potato Bites 26

T

Tasty "Banana" Nut Cake 19
Tasty Bagel Brussels Sprouts 31
Tasty Banana Bread Muffins 99
Tasty Cauliflower Pizza Crusts 91
Tasty Ranch Roasted Almonds 85
Tasty Roasted Sweet Potatoes 34
Tasty Seared Ribeye 77
Tasty Three-Berry Dutch Pancake 17
Tender Blackened Steak Nuggets 72
Tender Pork Spare Ribs 77
Teriyaki Chicken and Broccoli Bowls 61
Teriyaki Chicken Wings 58
Thinly Sliced Beef Jerky 83
Three-Meat Pizza 89
Thyme Roasted ChickenThyme Roasted Chicken 58
Turkey Burgers 60
Turkey-bread Meatballs 62

V

Vanilla and Cinnamon Roll sticks 23
Vanilla Extract and Lemon Poppy Seed Cake 19
Vanilla Pancake Cake 21
Veggie Cream Frittata 20
Versatile Bacon Potatoes with Green Beans 27
Versatile Potato Salad 35

W

Wonderful Parmesan French Fries 31
Wrapped Pork Tenderloin 67

Z

Zest Fried Aasparagus 30
Zesty Lemon-Caper Salmon Burgers 48

Printed in Great Britain
by Amazon